Dalton-in-Furness

Mediaeval Capital to Mining Community

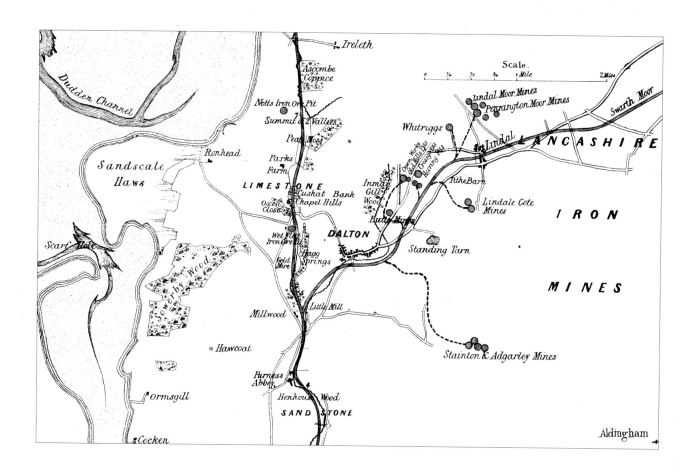

The story of the ancient capital of Furness and
the influences which gave it importance

Rock Battye

CUMBRIAN
RAILWAYS
ASSOCIATION

Front Cover

Main Picture - Sharp Stewart 2-4-0 locomotive No. I brings a workmen's train into Dalton station's down platform in the early years of the 20th century. (From a painting by Mike Spooner)

Title Page - James Walker's plan of 1843 for a railway to link the slate quarries at Kirkby and the iron mines around Dalton with shipping facilities at Barrow and Piel (see also Page 10). (Barrow Record Office ZK 45)

Back Cover

Top - English, Welsh & Scottish Railways Class 66 No. 66 169 heads a train of new rails from the Corus plant at Workington round the curve from Park South to Dalton Junction on 10 April 2003. (Alan Johnstone AJ-03-4982)

Middle Right - A First TransPennine Express Class 185 Desiro unit passing through Dalton station on a driver-training run on 2 February 2006. (Alan Johnstone AJ-06-2475)

Middle Left - The Coat of Arms of Dalton-in-Furness. The design is based upon two elements, both of which reinforce Dalton's historical links with Furness Abbey. The sword and the scales it supports represent the authority of the Abbot of Furness to dispense justice within his demesne from his court room at Dalton Castle. The stylised sheep hide represents the wealth which the Abbey accrued from the wool trade. (Dalton with Newton Town Council)

Bottom - The I p.m. Barrow-London blasts out of Dalton, with Class 5 4-6-0 No. 44761 piloting 'Jubilee' class 4-6-0 no. 45689 Ajax in March 1960. (Author)

Foldout Pages 67 & 68 - Drawings of Dalton station buildings on the Up Platform, the platform canopies and the footbridge in its later form. (From plans in the Barrow Record Office)

Text © R Battye and the Cumbrian Railways Association 2006

Maps © Cumbrian Railways Association 2006

Photographs © as credited

**Published by the Cumbrian Railways Association,
104 Durley Avenue, Pinner, Middlesex. HA5 IJH
The Association is a Registered Charity No. 1025436
www.cumbrianrailwaysassociation.co.uk**

Membership Secretary, 36 Clevelands Avenue, Barrow-in-Furness, Cumbria. LA13 0AE

Design and layout by Alan Johnstone,
24 Hartington Street, Barrow-in-Furness, Cumbria. LA14 5SL
Printed by Lamberts Print & Design, Settle, North Yorkshire

ISBN 0-9540232-4-2

CONTENTS

This book is dedicated to

the miners and quarrymen of Dalton and district for their fortitude and courage

An aerial view of Dalton-in-Furness from the south-east, taken in the 1950s. The cricket field and Railway Meadow are prominent. The Parish Church of St Mary is visible on the left of the picture. In the centre is Dowdales School, with Elliscales Farm beyond, while the Salvation Army Citadel can be seen on the right. In the distance is the Duddon Estuary, with the lower slopes of Black Combe just discernible. The main railway line sweeps across the front of the photograph, while the Stainton branch begins its steep climb through the cutting.
(Author's collection)

Introduction

I was born and brought up in Dalton, in a house which looked across the town to the railway station, a brisk five-minute walk away. The 'tang, tang' of hammer on anvil in the blacksmith's smithy nearby, the deep-throated 'ruff, ruff' of the Fowler-designed goods engines as they lifted a heavy freight up the bank, these are two of the sounds that have remained in my memory of those early years spent in the town.

There were happy childhood wanderings around Mouzell and Elliscales, where I could see the formation of the old railway lines that had served the iron mines in those areas. 'Stainton Bobby' still pushed its load of empty wagons up the hill to the limestone quarries in Stainton. There were many in Dalton who remembered the old times, and you could hear some fascinating tales being recounted by the 'old stagers' as they whiled away their days sitting on the seats at the 'Weint' corner.

Standing in the middle of Greystone Lane (as you could then, without fear of injury), it was interesting to note the line of the old road, leading past the cottages and over the railway line into Railway Terrace. And again, when the line left Dalton, it seemed to be heading for the coal drops at Crooklands before veering sharply right and making for Lindal Tunnel. The OS maps confirmed both of these sightings, but I was curious to know why. This curiosity partly explains the writing of this book.

One other sound of Dalton that still remains is of the bells of St Mary's Church, a ring of ten which attracts enthusiasts from far and near. This is a timely reminder of the early influence of the Church on the district, and, in particular, the prosperity which proximity to Furness Abbey brought to the town and which enabled it to become 'The Capital of Furness'.

Rock Battye
Staffordshire
May 2005

What tales they could tell! Six elderly gentlemen enjoy a pint at the Weint, celebrating, it is thought, the installation of the first seat at this popular corner for exchanging gossip.   (courtesy James Walton)

Furness Abbey established; life under the abbey; Scottish raiders and the Black Death; the Dissolution and after; the Plague and the Civil War

The ruins of Furness Abbey from the north-east, a 19th century view.   *(From Richardson's* Furness Past and Present)

The event which set Dalton on the road to becoming the mediaeval capital of Furness occurred on 16 July 1127, when Stephen, Earl of Boulogne and Moreton, afterwards to become King of England, gave land to enable a monastery to be set up. The lands were extensive:

all Furness and Walney, with the privilege of hunting; with Dalton, and all my lordship in Furness with the men and everything thereunto belonging, that is in woods and in open grounds, in land and in water; and Ulverston, and Roger Braithwaite and all that belongs to him; my fisheries at Lancaster, and Little Guoring, with all the land thereof.

So runs the charter which led to Abbot Ewan establishing a Benedictine monastery of 'Grey Monks' in the Valley of Deadly Nightshade about a mile and a half from Dalton, and it is signed by Henry, King of England, and Archbishop Thurston of York among other notables.

In those days there was no national lottery to help fund good causes, and kings and noblemen would endow schools, colleges, cathedrals, abbeys and such like. The benefactors knew that in this way their names would be remembered down the ages, and they could expect to be prayed for by those who had gained from their generosity. Stephen himself was quite honest about his motives, and early in the charter explains that he is:

providing for the safety of my own soul, the soul of my wife, the Countess Matilda, the soul of my lord and uncle, Henry, King of England and Duke of Normandy, and for the souls of all the faithful, living as well as dead.

The abbot moved with his monks from Tulketh, on the outskirts of Preston, where they had been for the previous four years, and began the work of establishing a community in Furness. Twenty years on, the emerging monastery was swallowed up by a more powerful order of monks, the Cistercians. Out went the grey habits, to be replaced by the white of their new Order.

It must not be thought that the new arrivals in Furness were men entirely given to devotional and scholarly activities. True, the daily offices would be sung and the academic work carried out, but there would only have been about thirty so occupied. Several hundred, however, would have been engaged in those secular activities essential to the efficient running of the monastery, for example, producing food, looking after the sick, and extending hospitality to the abbey's visitors.

At this time, Barrow was not even on the map; the first mention of 'Barrai' was in 1190, as a 'grange' or 'home farm' founded by the monks of the abbey. Its time would certainly come, but for that it would have to wait until well into the 19th century. Ulverston was a town of comparable size to

5

Dalton, but not as well situated, being about six and a half miles from the abbey. As a result, Dalton was the place to benefit because of its closer proximity.

The benefits indeed were considerable. Every week the tenants would take away from the abbey sixty barrels of beer (ten gallons in each barrel), and with each barrel a dozen loaves of bread. They had manure for their fields, iron for their farm equipment, and timber to repair their houses. They could send their children to receive an education in the monastery school. Certainly, they had obligations to the abbot, as had all tenants to their lord. But the benefits they received at least equalled those obligations.

Beside all this, there were important benefits to the community as a whole. The monks were well skilled in husbandry, and the tenants learned from them the more up-to-date and efficient methods of crop cultivation. Little Mill was one of several mills set up to enable them to grind their corn. Poaka Beck, the stream flowing past the town of Dalton and through the grounds of the abbey, was a useful source of power for these mills. Little Mill itself was situated near the foot of Mill Brow, close to where the railway now runs.

The ore was taken to the woods and forests of High Furness, where whole hillsides were cleared of trees to make the charcoal needed for smelting.

On the cleared hillsides the monks kept sheep, and maintained a lively export trade in good quality fleeces from their harbour on Piel Island. At times their business enthusiasm could land them in trouble, as when, in 1423, French merchants complained that the monks had tried to evade customs with a load of wool bound for Flanders, a polite way of saying that they were smuggling.

The monks had not been many years in Furness when a dispute arose between the abbey and the baron of Kendal concerning the boundary line between the Furness Fells and the barony. By command of King Henry II, the matter was referred to thirty sworn men. Before these witnesses the abbot divided the disputed lands by a line which ran down through Coniston Water and along the course of the River Crake. Invited to make his choice, the baron, William de Lancaster, selected the westernmost portion. For this he was to pay the abbey a yearly rent of twenty shillings, his son doing homage for it to the abbot. He also secured *the*

Furness Abbey from the west, a 19th century view.   *(From Richardson's* Furness Past and Present*)*

Also, the district around Dalton was rich in iron ore, whose existence had been known for many years. One William de Merton (Marton) gave some of his lands to the abbey monks

> of the Blessed Mary of Furness that they and
> their successors for ever may be able freely to dig
> mine or work for ore in 400 acres of land of the
> aforesaid William with the appurtenances in
> Dalton Orgrave and Merton ... and to throw out
> and raise all manner of mineral or ore there found
> out of the mines.

privilege of hunting and hawking on the abbey's lands to the east; doubtless hunting rights were the principal reason for the dispute.

In 1239 the town gained its royal charter, the first in Furness, which enabled it to hold a weekly market and an annual fair, which was initially at the Feast of All Saints but soon transferred to the Feast of St Edward the Confessor. With the abbot's secular court established in the town, Dalton was plainly much dependent on the abbey for its well-being and prosperity, and was indisputably the capital of the region during this period.

It must not be supposed that it was an idyllic existence living in the shadow of the abbey. The times were hard, and life expectancy was short. In the 14th century, two events in particular were to shake the town. The first of these involved two unwelcome visits of marauding Scotsmen from across the border. As the *Chronicle of Lanercost* notes, in 1316 a formidable army advanced westwards from Richmond in Yorkshire

> *laying waste everything as far as Furness, and burnt that district whither they had not come before, taking away with them all the goods of that district, with men and women as prisoners. Especially were they delighted with the abundance of iron which they found there, because Scotland is not rich in iron.*

Six years later the Scots were back again. This time the raiders were led by the redoubtable Robert the Bruce. Though his father's body was buried at Holme Cultram, that monastery was mercilessly plundered. While the good folk of Furness waited fearfully to learn their fate, the abbot thought he might try a little bribery. As the chronicler goes on:

> *But the abbot of Furness went to meet him and paid ransom for the district of Furness that it should not again be burnt or plundered and took him to Furness Abbey.*

There Robert was treated to a lavish display of hospitality. However, this cut little ice with the rank and file of the soldiery. So despite the abbot's best endeavours, the Scots behaved as before, and once more Dalton suffered. Again, it was the iron that was the prize, for the Scotsmen

> *seized all the manufactured iron they could find and carried it off with the greatest joy though so heavy of carriage, and preferred it to all other plunder.*

As a consequence of these raids, the abbot erected the Castle or Pele Tower in the town, still to be seen. Fortunately, it has never been called upon to fulfil its intended purpose of defence against the Scots.

Of the second event that afflicted the town, evidence is sparse. The epidemic of plague known as the Black Death came over from the continent. Originating in the east, by 1346 it had settled in the Tartar lands of Asia Minor. While besieging the Genoese trading port of Caffa (now Feodosiya) on the Crimean coast, a Tartar army found itself stricken with the plague. To give the good citizens a taste of the agony they were suffering, they used their giant catapults to lob over the city walls the corpses of the victims. The inhabitants speedily took to their galleys and fled, crossing the Black Sea towards the Mediterranean. Unfortunately, they carried the plague with them. It spread throughout the continent of Europe, arriving in England in 1348, and by 1349 it had reached at least as far north as Carlisle. Furness Abbey must have been affected very considerably, since the number of monks was so reduced that the refectory and dormitory had to be cut down in size. As much of the traffic to the abbey passed through Dalton, it is highly probable that the town suffered similarly. Because so little was known about the disease, it was probably an enemy to be feared even more than the Scots.

Picking themselves up from these calamities, Daltonians no doubt got on with the business of rebuilding the town and re-establishing themselves. The Wars of the Roses left Furness unscathed. In 1485, Henry Tudor defeated the Yorkist king, Richard III, at Bosworth and took the crown as Henry VII. He married Elizabeth of York, hoping by this means to unite both the warring factions. However, there were still some Yorkists who felt aggrieved, and they put up two pretenders, Lambert Simnel and Perkin Warbeck.

It is Lambert Simnel who concerns us in Furness. This eleven-year-old son of an Oxford baker was put up as Edward Plantaganet, Earl of Warwick, heir to the House of York. While the real earl languished in the Tower of London, Lambert Simnel arrived from Ireland in 1487 with considerable support, berthing his ships in Piel harbour on 4 June. Some two thousand German mercenaries and a considerable number of Irish soldiers spent the night at Swarthmoor before marching through Yorkshire and on towards London, where the army met defeat near Warwick. The young Simnel was captured. Henry, realising that he was just a pawn in the game, decided merely to make an example of him and put him to work in the Royal kitchens. The young pretender subsequently became one of the king's falconers. (In the similar subsequent uprising, Perkin Warbeck was treated less leniently, and was hanged after his defeat.)

Of Simnel's time at Piel, many legendary stories are told, involving trapdoors, haunted passageways and gruesome spectres, best left, perhaps, to the reader's imagination.

After this excitement had passed, the next few years or so continued to be relatively calm and peaceful, and with the help of the abbey, Dalton continued to keep its place as the market town of Furness. But this was to change dramatically.

The downfall of the monasteries is often seen as an act of King Henry VIII to deliberately flout the Pope while at the same time increasing his own wealth substantially. But abbots were men of power, and the corruption of powerful men is not a new phenomenon. At the beginning of the 16th century, the Abbot of Furness was Alexander Bankes. He seems to have been a thoroughly unpleasant character. Headstrong and domineering, he had sour relations with his land-owning neighbours and with his own tenants. He tried to deprive the king of £250 from a royal subsidy he had collected, and he obtained a pardon for a relation of his who had been convicted of murder. A man less fit to be the spiritual and pastoral leader of a monastery is hard to imagine. This sort of behaviour was unlikely to recommend itself to Henry.

When Abbot Alexander died, the king, no doubt indulging in a little careful forward planning, himself appointed Roger Pele to the position. Roger was a completely different character from his predecessor, weak, indecisive, and very concerned for his own safety. Consequently, when the king's commissioners arrived and asked him to surrender his monastery, he agreed with alacrity, to be granted the profits from the rectory of Dalton which had now passed to the crown, and coming to reside at the vicarage. (The Revd Christopher Cardale, when Vicar of Dalton, used to tell his confirmation class that, by rights, the vicar was still technically the Abbot of Furness, and that we might therefore show him a little more respect. His tongue, needless to say, was very firmly in his cheek!)

The Great Seal of Furness Abbey.
(From Richardson's Furness Past and Present*)*

The Deed of Surrender was signed on 9 April 1537 in the Chapter House of Furness Abbey, bringing to an end its 410-year existence. The effect on the town must have been devastating, its one big employer and major source of business wiped out at a stroke. Many would have been out of work, while others would find the demand for their goods and services considerably reduced. Farmers neglected the growing of grain, turning instead to cattle breeding; it would

be another two hundred years or so before agriculture in the district properly recovered. The weekly market declined, and Ulverston, whose own market charter dates from 1280, felt encouraged to set up a market in its place. Dalton became a sleepy backwater, while Ulverston thrived.

Plague struck the town in 1631, started, it seems, by a quack doctor called Lancaster and his wife who arrived from London. In treating the unfortunate victims, his 'cures' compounded their suffering, causing them to die in agony. In the seven months the plague was raging, over three hundred townspeople died, around half of Dalton's population. The perpetrators were eventually run out of town. The whole sad business was chronicled by the parish clerk, George Postlethwaite. This is how he recorded the end of the affair:

> *The pest bearer did not go off unrevenged by the hands of the women, who having vigilantly watched the gates and roads, assaulted him with stones which severely wounded his head, and then contended with crooked staffs. To those by whom the wounds were inflicted (but not without cause), the false, abandoned Lancaster pretended he was killed, and feigned not to inspire air, for the cunning rascal laid upon the ground as if he were dead, and thus the villain finally evaded the vengeance of the women and fled, which was pleasant and gave great joy to all.*

Both the minister, the Revd Richard Thomlinson, and his clerk had forsaken Dalton during this difficult time. Perhaps this explains the number of instances of Sabbath-breaking just after his return: Walter Preston *loytering in ye churchyard at service time and being admonished by ye churchwardens*

Norman Arch, Chapter House, Furness Abbey.

(From Richardson's Furness Past and Present*)*

Dalton church, the parsonage and the Castle, 'from an old picture'. (From Richardson's *Furness Past and Present)*

wold neither go in nor out; Jo. Knipe and William Peell *bowling upon ye Sabboath day in ye afternoone*; William Fether *gardinge* (gardening) *in time of Divine service in ye afternoon*; John Singleton and Thomas Woodburn *playing at pigles* (probably a version of the game of guinea pig) *upon Sunday in ye afternoon in time of Divine Service.* At any rate, like the Vicar of Bray, Thomlinson kept his post throughout the period of the Commonwealth following the Civil War and after the return of the Monarchy in 1660.

The well-known battles of the Civil War, Marston Moor, Naseby and Stow-on-the-Wold, were fought far away from Furness. While it might be said that Marston Moor secured the north for the Parliamentarians, there were, nevertheless, minor skirmishes, often involving the local gentry, and no fewer than two of these could qualify as the Battle of Dalton.

The first took place in the late summer of 1643. A Royalist force under the command of Colonel Sir William Huddleston established its headquarters at Dalton. The colonel arrested a number of Parliamentarians and imprisoned them in Dalton Castle. His security plainly left a great deal to be desired, for some of his prisoners escaped, and were able to take a warning to a Parliamentary force under Colonel Rigby, at that time besieging Thurland Castle, near Kirkby Lonsdale. He at once marched with his men

to Ulverston, covering the thirty miles or so over difficult terrain in one day. Setting off for Dalton the next morning, he met and soundly defeated the Royalists on the outskirts of the town. His work done, he returned to Thurland, leaving behind a troop of horse and a company of foot. As might be expected, they did Dalton no little harm before they eventually departed.

The second battle for Dalton levelled the score somewhat. After the Battle of Marston Moor on 2 July 1644, the defeated Royalist, Prince Rupert, sent Sir John Mayne into Furness, and he established his headquarters at Dalton. Anchored in Piel harbour lay part of the Parliamentary fleet; a number of sailors joined up with some of the local inhabitants and made their way to Dalton with the aim of driving him out. They met Sir John's forces when they were about a mile out of the town, and paid the price for their rash and foolish act; they were utterly routed, with two hundred prisoners taken besides many killed. Sir John and his forces retired to Holker, but were eventually obliged to leave the district.

Dalton once again settled down and carried on with its life. Soon, however, was to come a different kind of revolution, which would completely change the nature of the town and of the district.

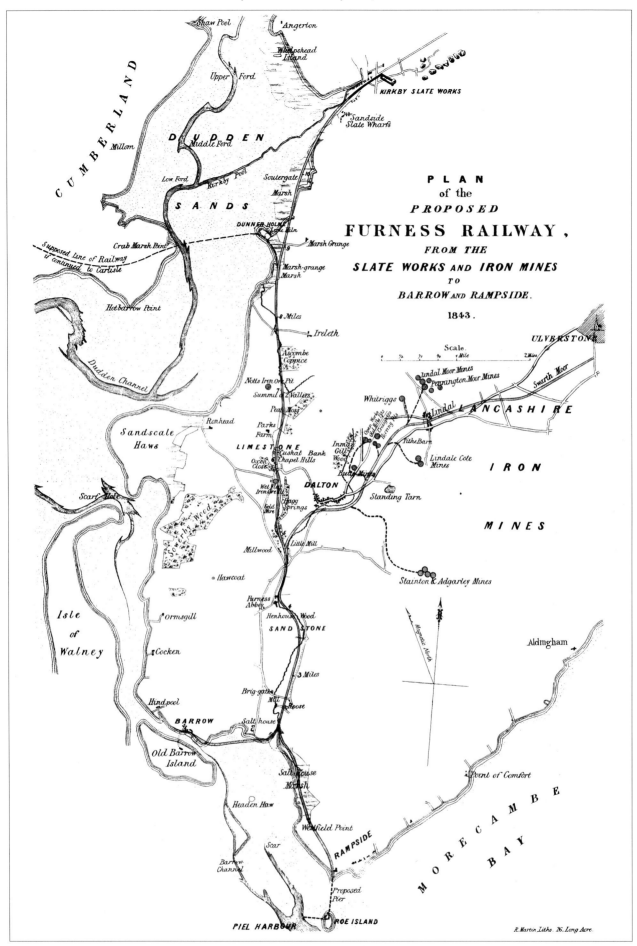

James Walker's plan of 1843 for a railway to link the slate quarries at Kirkby and the iron mines around Dalton with shipping facilities at Barrow and Piel.

(Barrow Record Office ZK 45)

Early iron ore mining; 'in the Bloomery way'; advances in the mining industry; conditions in the town; Henry Schneider; the coming of the railway

Ore-loading in progress near Conishead Priory, 1833.   (*From* Furness and The Industrial Revolution *by J D Marshall*)

Visitors to Cumbria often remark on the great contrasts in the geography that exist, with the forbidding crags and towering mountains of the central Lake District giving way to gentler green hills and more open, easy pastures of the surrounding regions. Many notice the varied geology also: the green slate, as at Kirkstone or Coniston, the red sandstone, as at Hawcoat or St Bees, and the white limestone, particularly common in the Furness area.

Within this limestone, iron ore in the form of haematite, a deep, rich red in colour, could often be found. This must have been well known to the monks of Furness Abbey, for the sites they selected to mine for ore were generally those where the limestone outcrops to the surface.

As the seventeenth century gave way to the eighteenth, there were at least five iron ore pits in the district, at Tytup, Marton Hills, Crossgates, Heaning Wood and Adgarley. The method of extraction was to dig a bell-shaped pit, narrower at the top than at the bottom. These could not be very large, even with timber supports, for there was always the risk of rock falls from the unstable soil above the taper.

The ore was an oxide of iron, and to isolate the iron it would be smelted using some form of carbon, in a chemical reaction that might be written simply as:

oxide of iron + carbon → iron + oxide of carbon (gas)

The form of carbon favoured was charcoal. Familiar nowadays as a fuel for the barbecue, it is produced by machine. Then, it was a long and difficult process, with success not always guaranteed. The coppice woods of High Furness provided young saplings (sixteen or seventeen years old).

These were cut into billets, and arranged around a central stake; this was removed when the heap was complete to form a central chimney. The wood was covered with layers of small brushwood and turf, the object being to burn the wood in a reduced supply of oxygen. After firing, and when burning was sufficiently advanced, the chimney top was closed with turf. The combustion had to be carefully watched, and any flames smothered out with earth and gravel or with water. It was a long, slow process, over two or three days, because a slower burn gave a better quality of charcoal. Irvine Hunt's poem, *The Charcoal Burners*, describes the process romantically but accurately, and leads to a happy outcome:

> *... suddenly tired men regain their drive*
> *as in each mind the thought prevails:*
> *Has it worked; had the burn gone well?*
> *Slowly, the cooled mound is turned back.*
> *The tired burners smile. The prize, the charcoal,*
> *glistens satin-black, and rings clear as a bell.*

The smelting process itself took place in a clay-lined furnace. Charcoal was placed on the clay base, and then alternate layers of charcoal and ore embedded in charcoal were added, with small charcoal pounded firm on top of the pile. Fire was introduced into the furnace, and a blast of air turned on by means of bellows. The oxygen blown in combined with the carbon of the incandescent charcoal, and was converted into carbon monoxide, a 'reducing gas'. The gas as it rose combined with the oxygen of the ore, producing the chemical change which reduced the ore to its metallic state. As the reduction took place at about

11

1200°C, somewhat below the melting point of iron (1528°C), only a partial reduction was effected, the iron retrieved from the furnace being called the 'bloom'. Because it still retained a high carbon content, the bloom at this stage was too brittle. To make the crude bloom fit for use by the blacksmith, it needed to be consolidated or 'forged' by repeated hammering, with intermittent re-heating.

Because the efficiency of these furnaces was low, it took a considerable amount of woodland to smelt even a small quantity of ore. Consequently, the bloomeries were situated in High Furness close to the supply of charcoal. The ore had to be transported there for smelting, which was not an easy matter. It was usual to cart the ore to the eastern Furness shore. Mines around Lindal would send theirs down the aptly-named Red Lane to Conishead, Bardsea or Baycliffe, while those from Adgarley would be likely to use Beanwell. Ships in ballast were floated on to the shore at high water. The ballast would then be unloaded and replaced by the waiting ore. The ships would be lifted off by the next high tide. If destined for the local ironworks, they could then complete their journey along the coast and up the River Leven, landing the ore close to the site of the bloomeries. Much of the ore went for processing elsewhere, however, and these ships would sail southwards, often to ironworks in South Wales. Iron ore from Dalton was noted being processed at ironworks in the Wye Valley above Tintern Abbey by one Stebbing Shaw, touring the West of England in 1788.

While timbered bell-pits remained the norm in the case of the shallower mining, as these deposits began to be worked out it was necessary to sink deeper and deeper shafts in order to exploit the mineral. One such shaft sunk in 1728 on Adgarley Green was about 36 feet deep, and there was a passage or 'drift' 35 feet long linking to an earlier shaft. It could be worked by three men: the hewer, who split the rock with wedges and broke the ore with his pick, another to cut and fix the timber to support the roof of the drift, and a third who raised the ore to the surface. At this pit a 'horse gin', was in use, in which a horse plodded round in a circle to turn a capstan which had a rope wrapped around it. This was necessarily some little distance from the shaft, so the rope was then taken over a pulley or beam at the mouth of the shaft. Other pits were more primitive and used a jackroll, a stout timber beam about ten inches in diameter suspended in a frame and placed diagonally across the mouth of the shaft in the manner of the traditional well mechanism. Iron handles at each end were turned by manpower.

As shafts were sunk deeper and deeper, flooding became a problem, inevitably so in Furness with its high water table. With nothing other than manpower, horsepower or waterpower to assist, the rag and chain pump was perhaps the best solution. Usually water-powered, these had an iron chain, broadened at intervals by knobs of cloth stiffened with leather, and turned around a rag-wheel. This was furnished with iron spikes to keep the chain steady. The knobs forced up the water, which was then channelled away from the mine workings. There were many pits in Furness not aspiring to anything as sophisticated as that, where wooden or cast-iron buckets called kibbles were used for raising the water.

George Romney. (From Richardsons's Furness Past & Present*)*

A cabinet-maker named Romney working in Dalton was engaged in the construction of pumps for use in the local mines. He had a son, George, born at Beckside on 15 December 1734. After schooling at Dendron, George helped his father who was now farming an estate at Cocken. Here George developed a talent as a carver and guilder, constructing violins and flutes. At the age of 21, he was apprenticed to a travelling portrait painter named Steel, and went with him to Kendal. George Romney went on to make a name for himself as a painter in London, being especially well known for his portraits of Lady Hamilton. Perhaps Dalton's best-known son, he died in 1802, being buried in Dalton churchyard. The gravestone can be seen today, refurbished but still in its original position.

At the beginning of the eighteenth century, all the local iron was made 'in the Bloomery way', but then in 1711, two charcoal iron companies established ambitious enterprises in the neighbourhood. Two off-comers from Cheshire, Edward Hall and Thomas Cotton, formed the Cunsey Company. This was naturally resented by the local ironmasters, William Rawlinson and John Machell, who set up a new company, the Backbarrow Iron Company, establishing new blast furnaces at Backbarrow (on the site of a former bloomery forge) and at Leighton, near Silverdale. Abraham Darby visited Furness in 1712, but, despite his visit and his experiments in coke-smelting, there is no evidence that any of the local companies attempted to use the coke-smelting process during the eighteenth century. He did, however, persuade the two rival firms to co-operate in a price-fixing arrangement. At this time the Backbarrow company was taking ore from Adgarley and Crossgates, and the two jointly worked Heaning Wood. Another company established itself in 1735, and later set up furnaces at Newland, near Ulverston.

As the eighteenth century went on, the output of iron ore steadily increased. The 1780s and 1790s were the peak years, with probably about 20,000 tons mined annually. Shortly before 1780, *the richest ore [was] found in immense quantities* at a pit in Adgarley. West goes on to say, in his *Guide to the Lakes*, that *one hundred and forty tons have been raised at one shaft in twenty-four hours*. These mines at Stainton were on land belonging to the Cavendish family. The Duke of Buccleuch owned several mines in the Lindal area; these too were doing well and producing around 12,000 tons a year at this time.

At the furnaces at Backbarrow and Leighton, production of small cast-iron ware increased, largely due to the work of Isaac Wilkinson, who was pot-founder at Backbarrow until 1748. Cast-iron pots, kettles and pans were produced in quantity, and in 1752, no fewer than 19,000 such articles were cast from 190 tons of pig-iron. Transhipment of the ore was improved when the Backbarrow Iron Company obtained an ore storage floor at Barrow in 1776. When the Newland company built a quay there soon afterwards, the effect was to reduce the cost of loading from 6s 6d to 1s 4d for twenty tons of ore. Although the Ulverston Canal was

opened in 1796, the operating company was not particularly co-operative towards the iron companies, and the freight charges were higher. Consequently Ulverston saw trade disappearing south through Dalton towards the new, small harbour at Barrow.

At this period, while Dalton did not have the influence it had in monastic times, nevertheless the parish was still a large one of some 27 square miles, containing the divisions of Dalton Proper (i.e. Dalton township), Above Town, Hawcoat (which included Walney) and Yarlside. Local government was in the hands of the 'Four and Twenty,' a self-electing authority consisting of twenty four sidesmen, six from each of the divisions.

Although this chapter has been largely concerned with the early development of the iron ore mines, in fact the region was predominantly agricultural. Methods were not very advanced; in 1772 the inhabitants of the area had *but recently applied themselves to husbandry*. Furthermore, *till within these twenty years even the use of dung was scarcely known to them*. But the glacial clays provided a soil very suitable for wheat growing, and towards the end of the century the district was recognised as one of the few wheat-growing

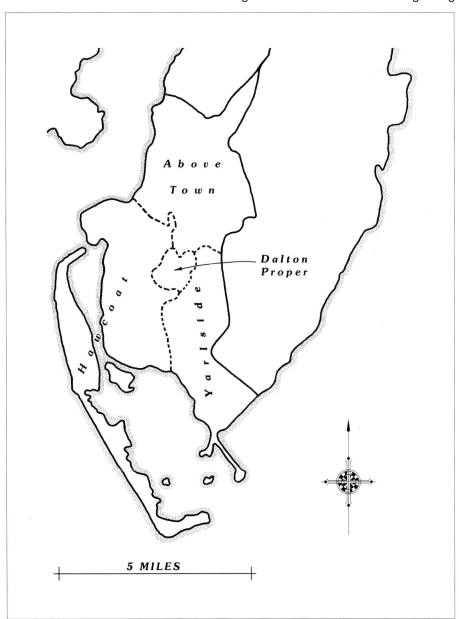

Map of the area, showing the extent of Dalton Parish, with the four Divisions.
(Author / Alan Johnstone)

areas of Lancashire. Barley was also important, with the harvested crop going to maltsters in Dalton and in Ulverston.

Farmers would augment their income in a number of ways. They would transport the ore from the mines, the carts used being larger and stronger than the usual farm carts. Though this took place all the year round, they preferred to work in the winter, when work on the farm was slack and the ground was hard, making the roads less likely to become churned up with mud. The slate quarries at Kirkby, which from 1773 became part of the Cavendish estates, had their sites rented out. Some local farmers took advantage of this, finding their profits were about double the rent which they paid. Despite this, sons of farmers found it difficult to continue in farm work, and had *generally been bound apprentices to such mechanical employments as are indispensable in the country.*

William Fisher was a yeoman farmer or 'statesman' working about 85 acres of land close to the Barrow Channel, still at this time in the Parish of Dalton. His diary records the sowing of wheat, barley and oats, the growing of potatoes, beans and peas, and the keeping of dairy cattle to make butter and cheese. There were good and bad years. The entry for 13 July 1821 reveals: *had got all our Meddow hay without any Rain been very hot and dry weather,* and in 1831 reports *a very fine Harvest.* However, disaster struck in 1834, when the wheat was a failing crop *from the wetness of the Weather.*

Wages in the slate quarries were good for the skilled worker. In 1793, for example, while a general labourer in the ore mines would be earning about 1s 6d a day, *those who are expert at riving or chopping slate* [are] *making £50 or £60 a year each.* This compares well with wages for those in domestic service, where men servants could expect to receive about £16 a year and women servants £5.

Some of the slate from the quarries found its way to Dalton. One writer stated, in 1805, that the town is *much improved of late, many of the worst houses having been pulled down and rebuilt in a plain and neat manner and covered with slate.* The writer was the town's medical practitioner, Dr William Close. The son of a Walney farmer, he had trained in Edinburgh before coming to Dalton to practise in 1797. He was well advanced for his time, introducing vaccine inoculations against smallpox into Furness in 1799, only one year after Edward Jenner had publicised it, and remarked that *the inhabitants of Furness are very healthy.* He was a man of many talents, editing the second edition of Thomas West's *Antiquities of Furness* and patenting a polyphonic trumpet. William Fisher's diary entry for 15 May 1813 records: *Doctor Close Departed this Life in the 39 year of his age much and Deserved Lamented by all who knew him.*

At the beginning of the nineteenth century, the effects of steam power began to be felt. The first uses of steam were in the construction of pumps, essential for the working of the mines as they sank deeper and deeper shafts in search of further mineral deposits. Newcomen had built his first successful pumping engine, under the patent of Capt. Thomas Savery, and installed it at a colliery at Tipton, near Dudley, in the Midlands. The engine was called a 'beam engine', since it used a massive oak beam, pivoted at the centre, which

The Little Mill in winter, in the 19th century. The railway has reached Dalton, for on the right can be seen the signal cabin at Millwood Junction, the tall signals and a train just coming into view from the direction of Furness Abbey.

(From Richardson's Furness Past and Present*)*

Dalton Castle and Market Cross, showing some of the houses with slate roofs, c. 1827.
(Cumberland, Westmorland and Lancashire Illustrated, *T H A Fielding*)

transferred the upward motion of the piston rod at one end of the beam into the downward motion of the pump crank at the other. James Watt and Matthew Boulton worked hard to improve the breed, but, as so often happens, the technology was lagging behind the ideas. Here, what was needed was improved accuracy in boring out the cylinders. The problem was solved by John 'Iron-Mad' Wilkinson, son of the pot-founder Isaac already mentioned, and by now a successful ironmaster in the Midlands. By modifying his cannon boring machinery, he had the cylinder casting fixed upon a supporting frame. The revolving cutter bar passed right through the casting, being supported by bearings at both ends, and in this way, he was able to produce a cylinder bore that was both circular and parallel.

These engines were inexpensive to buy and very simple in operation, but they were inefficient and burnt large quantities of coal. This was of little account to colliery owners in the north-east of England, since they had plenty of waste, second-rate coal to burn. For the owners of Cornish tin mines, however, it was another story altogether, since there was no local coal and transport costs were high. Richard Trevithick, a Cornish engineer, produced a more efficient design, a single-acting condensing engine operating at a much higher steam pressure. This became very popular in Cornwall and became known as a 'Cornish' pumping engine. It was, in time, installed in all parts of the world, as well as in mining areas in Britain where fuel was scarce. These engines would be seen in Furness in due course.

There was one London company with a wide range of commercial interests, both in England and overseas. With tin mines in Cornwall and coal mines in South Wales, this company had considerable experience of mining speculation and development. A son of the firm was, by the age of eighteen, already secretary of its associated company, the Mexican and South American Company, and he visited the English Lake District on holiday in 1839. His name was Henry Schneider.

Schneider lost no time in making the acquaintance of the leading mine owners of the district. At this time the firm of Harrison, Ainslie & Co. was mining at Lindal Moor, the Ulverston Mining Company was at Lindal Cote, while Thomas Fisher was at Butts Beck and Whitriggs. A particularly useful contact for Schneider was the Agent for the Earl of Burlington, Joseph Jopling, who also managed the Kirkby Slate Quarries. He encouraged Schneider, who began a series of expensive searches in various parts of the district, purchased Whitriggs Mine from Thomas Fisher, and set up the Furness Mining Company with its headquarters at Orgrave Mill, Dalton. If further evidence of his commitment to Furness were needed, William Fisher's diary provides it, for his entry of 16 September 1842 includes: *married on 14 Septr H W Schneider esq, of Southgate Middlesex to Augusta second daughter of Richard Smith of Bank field near Urswick.* (Richard Smith was a local ironmaster, a partner in the Ulverston Mining Company which was operating at Lindal Cote.)

Henry Schneider was not impressed with the methods of ore mining then in use; the ore was still being raised by jackroll or horse-gins, and there were *no pumps in the whole district, and, in fact, water, being reached, put a stop to further operations.* Under such primitive conditions, accidents were common. Subsidence and rock falls occurred regularly; William Fisher's diary entry for March 1827 reports *Thomas Sowerbuts killed at the Iorn Ore pits by the roof of the pit falling in.* Ventilation of the mine could be a problem and in 1828 two men were *Sufacated by the foul air* at Crossgates Pit, two other men with them fortunately able to escape by *accinding the Shaft in the bucket,* the usual method for raising and lowering miners at this time.

By now there were four piers for the loading of iron ore at Barrow. The oldest was close to the ford across the channel to Barrow Island, installed by the Newlands company in 1790 to replace their original and shorter pier. Another was erected in 1833 by Town & Rawlinson who were mining at Crossgates, and a further one in 1839 by the Ulverston Mining Company. The fourth was put up by Henry Schneider and his partners in 1842. Trade was very positively swinging away from Ulverston and towards the new and growing port of Barrow. Inevitably, the road to Barrow from the mines around Dalton was becoming extremely congested from the increasing number of ore carts travelling that way.

Henry Schneider was fully aware that transport problems were becoming acute, and he attempted to interest the Duke of Buccleuch in a tramway linking the mines with the port of Barrow. This was the second time such an idea had been mooted, and it met with as little success as the first. Undaunted, the mine owners engaged the Kendal engineer Job Bintley to survey possible routes from the Dalton iron mines to Barrow. One of the routes was by Sowerby Wood, the other and shorter route being through Furness Abbey and Newbarns, both intended for horse traction. Meanwhile, James Walker was reporting to the Earl of Burlington, owner of the slate quarries at Kirkby. Walker was a very distinguished man, President of the Institute of Civil Engineers at the time, so it was natural that, when the two interests combined, he it was who was asked to prepare a further report on a railway to serve both the iron mines and the slate quarries of the district. In his earlier report, he had referred favourably to Job Bintley's proposals, commenting that either route

> would be an immense improvement upon the present mode of conveyance, which is by one-horse carts upon very hilly roads that are cut up by it in the winter to the cost of the Parish of Dalton, which is bound to keep the roads in repair.

However, the subsequent proposals in his later report came out in favour of a line from Rampside to Kirkby, with a branch to Barrow, together with a line from a junction at Millwood passing to the north of the town of Dalton and proceeding through to Lindal Moor, the intention being to serve all the mines in the area.

These proposals were deemed satisfactory, and the Prospectus of the Furness Railway was published soon after. However, the line of route had been changed, passing to the south of Dalton and continuing to Crooklands and Lindal. With the Earl of Burlington and the Duke of Buccleuch prominent among the list of shareholders, the Furness Railway Bill received the Royal Assent on 23 May 1844. Dalton was about to be put on the railway map at last.

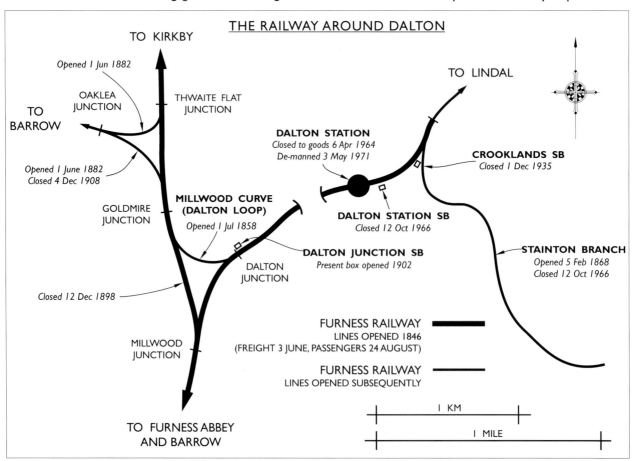

THE RAILWAY AROUND DALTON

TO KIRKBY

Opened 1 Jun 1882

OAKLEA JUNCTION

THWAITE FLAT JUNCTION

TO BARROW

*Opened 1 June 1882
Closed 4 Dec 1908*

TO LINDAL

DALTON STATION
*Closed to goods 6 Apr 1964
De-manned 3 May 1971*

CROOKLANDS SB
Closed 1 Dec 1935

GOLDMIRE JUNCTION

MILLWOOD CURVE (DALTON LOOP)
Opened 1 Jul 1858

DALTON STATION SB
Closed 12 Oct 1966

DALTON JUNCTION SB
Present box opened 1902

DALTON JUNCTION

STAINTON BRANCH
*Opened 5 Feb 1868
Closed 12 Oct 1966*

Closed 12 Dec 1898

MILLWOOD JUNCTION

FURNESS RAILWAY
LINES OPENED 1846
(FREIGHT 3 JUNE, PASSENGERS 24 AUGUST)

FURNESS RAILWAY
LINES OPENED SUBSEQUENTLY

TO FURNESS ABBEY AND BARROW

1 KM

1 MILE

Constructing the line; open for traffic; a description of the line; early days; mineral lines; Barrow Haematite Steel Co Ltd; further railway developments

Furness Railway locomotive No. 3. This locomotive entered service in 1846 and was withdrawn in 1900. Displayed for many years in a glass case outside Barrow Central station, she suffered shrapnel damage in the air raid of 4/5 May 1941. She is now safely preserved at the National Railway Museum in York.
(Mike Peascod collection)

The contractors for the line were Messrs John and William Treadwell, who constructed the formation 14 feet wide to allow for a double line of rails if this was subsequently found desirable. The contract only stipulated completion to Crooklands, just north of the town, as it was felt that the section through Lindal to Ulverston would prove unremunerative at that time. The workmen were expected to put in a ten-hour day: for this, labourers could earn 3s, while skilled masons could command 5s. A single line of iron rails was laid (steel rails were still some years in the future), under the supervision of Resident Engineer, Mr F C Stileman.

Work began in 1845, and it soon dawned upon the citizens of Dalton that there were to be level crossings close to the town. Led by Mr Baldwin, they presented a petition to the railway company, arguing against these. In vain did the company stress the many benefits which the railway would bring. It was a bridge they wanted, and eventually the company was obliged to build one near Goose Green at an extra cost of £2000.

By June, construction of the line had reached the grounds of Furness Abbey, and, that month, the Treadwells' labourers were observed during their dinner break among the abbey ruins. The observer was William Wordsworth. Impressed by the seemly behaviour of the workmen, but furious with the promoters for building the line so close to the abbey, he penned the lines:

Well have yon Railway Labourers to THIS ground
Withdrawn for noontide rest. They sit, they walk
Among the ruins, but no idle talk
Is heard; to grave demeanour all are bound;
And from one voice a Hymn with tuneful sound
Hallows once more the long-deserted Quire
And thrills the old sepulchral earth, around.
Others look up, and with fixed eyes admire
That wide-spanned arch, wondering how it was raised,
To keep, so high in air, its strength and grace:
All seem to feel the spirit of the place,
And by the general reverence God is praised:
Profane Despoilers, stand ye not reproved,
While thus these simple-hearted men are moved?

The behaviour of the navvies is hardly typical of their 'hard drinking, hard fighting' reputation, but many working on the Furness line would have been local men tempted to leave their existing employment for the higher wages on the railway. And in fairness to James Walker, his line of route carefully skirted the abbey grounds, passing through a short tunnel on its way towards Dalton.

By August, the Earl of Burlington could observe that *the line has made much progress, and in some parts is nearly finished.* However, these were the years of 'Railway Mania', causing something of a labour shortage, so construction had to continue through the following winter and into 1846.

The terrain was not difficult for the construction of the railway, but there were accidents, none the less. As William Fisher's diary for 1846 recounts, on 10 May:

> *Henry Houghton a youth 16 years of age unfortunately fell under one of the Waggons of the furness Railway and had his legs so much crushed that he died a few days after of inflamation,*

while on 16 July:

> *Wm Wilson a labourer on Furness railway 22 years of age who through inadvertance had placed Himself betwixt two Waggons one of which was moving when his knee was caught betwixt them which cosed acompound fracture ending in mortification and Died 7 days after.*

The Furness Railway had ordered a number of items of rolling stock for when the line was ready. There were four locomotives from the firm of Bury, Curtis & Kennedy. To a design by Edward Bury, one of the partners of the firm, these engines had the characteristic bar frames better able to cope with the poor trackwork of the time, and also the haystack-shaped copper fireboxes which led to the most famous of these four, No.3, being given the nickname 'Old Coppernob'. The only way to transport the locomotives was by sea, and they were sent over from Liverpool to be unloaded at Barrow. A popular account relates that, when the first such engine raised steam, it scared the life out of the local lads! There were some sixty wagons intended for the transport of iron ore, as well as ten further trucks for slate from the Kirkby quarries. Passengers were not totally neglected, four passenger carriages being purchased, but only for the use of 1st and 2nd class passengers. When it was realised that the lower orders were extremely keen to try this new form of transport, it was necessary for the company's carpenter to fit up some of the wagons with *neat deal seats.*

By June of 1846, the line was in a fit state to carry freight, and the first iron ore trains began running from Crooklands down the line to Barrow. The Lancaster Guardian suggested that, what with the trains beginning to run, the 'Whit Walks' taking place, and a large fair setting up, *the Dalton people will be likely to have a gay week of it.* The last section of line to be completed was that from Rampside Junction (Roose) to Roa Island.

With an early August opening date in view, the Board of Trade sent Major General C W Pasley, the Inspector General of the Railway Department, to examine the line. He arrived at Piel Pier on 3 August, having sailed over from Fleetwood on the steamer *Nile*. He travelled by train up the line to Dalton, noting that *the railway is good.* He went on to Kirkby and then to Barrow, finishing his tour at Furness Abbey where he enjoyed *collation with champagne.* His report recommended that the railway was safe to be opened for public use.

At the half-yearly General Meeting, the directors could report that:

> *The portion of the line between Dalton and Barrow has been partially opened for goods traffic, and the amount of iron ore carried since the opening has been equal to your Directors' anticipations considering that the full complement of waggons has, from unavoidable circumstances, not yet been delivered.*

They went on to say:

> *The remainder of the line having since been completed, its opening for passengers was sanctioned by the Board of Trade on the 12th instant* [12 August 1846].

The new line was a link in a chain whereby travellers arriving from the south at Preston could now be taken on to the new port of Fleetwood along the metals of the

Furness Railway 0-6-0 locomotive No. 4 leaving Dalton tunnel with a train for Barrow. The original tunnel portal can be seen.
(CRA Pattinson collection PA 0331)

The present portal seen after the reconstruction work of the 1950s. Class 5 4-6-0 No. 45386 emerges with a down local in 1958.

(Author)

Preston & Wyre Railway, opened in 1840. They could then take a steamer across to Piel, and use the new Furness Railway to Dalton, where a horse omnibus might take them to Ulverston and on to Newby Bridge. The only problem, the one weak link in the chain, was that Piel Pier belonged to one John Abel Smith, and he was anxious to cash in on the developing situation by persuading the railway company to use his new pier for shipping the iron ore. Unwilling to pay the tolls that Smith demanded, and preferring to use the jetties at Barrow instead, the company would not agree. Smith had promised to provide the steamer for the new service, but, because of the arguments and procrastinations, this was not ready. The other parties involved agreed to share the cost of chartering the *Ayrshire Lassie*, and, with the chain now complete, the first passenger train operated to Dalton on 24 August.

The Lancaster Guardian carried a substantial advertisement for the new service, which showed sailings from Fleetwood at 11 a.m. and 2 p.m. (11 a.m. only on Sundays) and from Piel at 1 p.m. and 4 p.m. (4 p.m. only on Sundays). The fare for the trip was 2s in the saloon and 1s on deck. On the arrival of the steamer, trains would leave Piel Pier for Furness Abbey and Dalton, returning in time for the steamer's next departure, leaving Dalton at 12.30 p.m. and 3.30 p.m. Fares between Piel Pier and Dalton or Furness Abbey were 1s First Class, 8d Second Class and 6d Third Class. Much was made of the 'conveyances' that took passengers on to Ulverston and to Newby Bridge where they could enjoy a trip on the Windermere Steam Yachts *Lord of the Isles* and *Lady of the Lake* to Bowness and Ambleside.

Before the week was out, the timetable had changed, with steamer departures from Fleetwood at 9 a.m. and 1.30 p.m.

and from Piel at 10.30 a.m. and 3 p.m. On Sundays there was the one sailing each way, from Fleetwood at 10.30 a.m. and from Piel at 3.30 p.m. This brought corresponding changes to the railway timetable, so that trains now left Dalton at 9.45 a.m. and 2.30 p.m. On 10 September, there was a further notice of change, with the afternoon sailing leaving Fleetwood at 12.45 p.m. and returning from Piel at 2.30 p.m., the afternoon train departure from Dalton being retimed to leave at 1.45 p.m. The Sunday sailing remained unchanged, but passengers still left Dalton at 1.45 p.m., giving them plenty of time to admire the delights of Piel before their boat sailed.

Coming up from Barrow, the line to Dalton diverged from the Kirkby line at Millwood Junction, quite close to the site of Little Mill, where a pointsman would be on duty. (To put the railway and steamer fares into some kind of perspective, his wages were 15s per week.) Pointsmen were obliged to remain alert and vigilant even during the worst weather, and it was some time before shelters were provided. Perhaps the tall, circular tower which once stood here, with its conical pointed roof, had been such a shelter. Reminding the writer O S Nock of a mediaeval watchtower on the Rhine, it would certainly have given the pointsman good visibility. The footpath from Dalton (the 'Low Road'), which runs past Little Mill and on to Furness Abbey, was soon crossed, at this time on the level. Climbing on a gradient of 1 in 101, the single-track line then passed under the Dalton to Barrow road before entering Dalton Tunnel. This tunnel, some 225 yards in length, had its sidewalls erected by James Garden, a builder who had just arrived in the district. He was to make his mark on the town in the not-too-distant future. The tunnel portals were quite attractive, with limestone arches and wing walls, and coursed masonry spandrels. The tunnel was only about 23 ft in diameter, and situated on a curve, and though built for double track, the clearances were to prove rather tight for the longer-wheelbased stock that would come in due time.

Emerging into daylight, the gradient eased to 1 in 308/151 as the line arrived at Dalton station. At this time there was very little in the way of facilities for intending passengers. A siding diverging to the left ran into a warehouse, while the main running line ran alongside a very low passenger platform. You would have looked in vain for a waiting room, sheltered platform canopy or any other conveniences. Things would improve somewhat once the directors began to appreciate the needs of passengers, but, when the line was first built, the movement of iron ore was of over-riding importance. Access to the station was from the road out of Dalton towards Stainton, which crossed the line on the level just before its junction with the road to Newton (Holly Gate Road). The railway line then continued climbing at 1 in 97 to Crooklands, where there were facilities for loading the ore wagons. The intention was to lay cheap tramlines from this point to the mines.

On 27 October, the Cumberland Pacquet could report:

> On this day week [20 October], the Furness line of Railway, which opened for traffic in July and passengers in August, was formally and publicly opened, and the event was celebrated by the directors with an excursion along the line, and a grand banquet at the Furness Abbey Station. In accordance with previous arrangements, the train, consisting of seven carriages, containing the Earl of Burlington, the Board of Directors, and a very numerous party of invited guests, left the Furness Station precisely at half past eleven o'clock, and proceeded along the line, which is fifteen miles in length, accompanied by the Kirkby Ireleth brass band, which greatly enlivened the scene. The train reached Dalton, the eastern terminus of the line, without the slightest drawback on the pleasant excursion, and after remaining a few minutes set out on its return to the Furness Abbey Station, and about sixty gentlemen sat down to a most excellent dinner, which was provided by Mr. Parker, of the Sun inn, Ulverston, and served up in the large room in the Manor House. The chair, on this occasion, was occupied by B. Currey Esq., chairman of the Board of Directors, who was supported right and left by the Earl of Burlington, the Directors, and a number of the most respectable gentlemen in the neighbourhood. The usual loyal and constitutional toasts having been disposed of, the after-dinner proceedings became extremely animated, and we are glad to observe that the necessity for extending this railway in a southerly direction was both universally admitted and generally advocated by the different speakers who addressed the meeting.

After the first six months of operation, the directors could feel well pleased with the results of their enterprise. Transport of the iron ore was noted as well managed, and receipts from Minerals, Merchandise, etc. were £4,639 10s 8d. The passenger service had only operated for two months, but in that short time it had attracted many visitors to Furness Abbey; as the Earl of Burlington somewhat ruefully remarked, after the train returns to Piel, the mob vanishes. To encourage the tourist trade, the company had purchased Furness Abbey Manor House from the Earl, and this was being converted into an hotel.

The warehouse and office at Dalton railway station were broken into on the night of 24 November 1848. The Ulverston Advertiser reported that:

> the effects therein contained had not been of a description to suit the depredators, as they departed without taking anything away.

This suggests that mere curiosity had got the better of some of the Dalton lads, and they had decided to see for themselves what this new-fangled railway business was all about.

To cope with the substantial traffic being generated, it was decided to double the line between Dalton and Rampside Junction, and its successful completion was reported to the directors at the next half-yearly meeting on 28 August 1847. The following year the directors were stressing that the Mineral and Goods Traffic shall be primarily . . . provided for, with passengers merely an auxiliary source of profit. Nevertheless, Bradshaw showed three trains per day operating in March 1850, the little 'Bury' locomotives taking half an hour for the non-stop run between Barrow and Dalton. Passengers of all classes, 1st, 2nd and 3rd, were provided for on all trains.

The Whitehaven & Furness Junction Railway was opening up the Cumbrian coast. Connecting with the Furness Railway's metals now extended to Broughton, this line opened throughout on 1 November 1850. This did away with the difficult crossing by coach of the treacherous Duddon sands, making travelling considerably easier; William Fisher's diary records that, on 23 January, 1853:

> Richard Fisher [William's eldest son] with his 2 Brothers in law went by Train to Wthaven and to New Monkwray attended the Sale of John Briggs on the 24th and a sale near Harrington on the 25th returned home on the 26th.

Goods became cheaper also, and Daltonians could obtain coal, transported from the West Cumberland coalfield, at a cost of 11s 3d a ton in the town. The impact of the railway on business at that time must have been similar to that of the Internet in our own day.

By now the directors had begun to take passenger traffic a little more seriously and purchased two small 2-2-2 well-tank locomotives to supplement the little 'Bury' engines. For it was not only business people who benefited by the new form of transport. On 14 August of the same year, William Fisher had visitors:

> Mrs Parker with her son and his Wife two Grandsons and a Grandaughter also Miss A Clark came from Ulverstone by [horse-drawn] Buss and Rail to see us.

However, while freight may have been declared to be of prime importance, substantial mining interests on Lindal Moor were still separated from the railway by the limestone cliffs at Crooklands, and they were impatient to see progress. The contract for the section of line from Crooklands to

Crooklands in the mid-1930s, looking towards Lindal, with the site of the ore-loading bank in the centre of the picture. The circular building was believed to be, at various times, a limestone crushing plant, a stable for the horses working the mineral lines, and a miners' 'dry'.

(CRA Pattinson collection PA0239)

Lindal had been awarded as far back as 1847, but the insolvency of the contractors, Wheatcroft, held up the work. The wet winter of 1850/51 caused further delays, and the line was not brought into operation until the summer of 1851. Further extension of the line to Ulverston was accomplished in 1854. William Fisher's youngest son, Henry, then living in Whitehaven, lost no time in making use of the new extension, for on 22 December, the diary records:

> *Henry came to Dalton went to Uston [Ulverston]*
> *next day and came to Barrow that night.*

Meanwhile, a substantial amount of ore was being carted to the ore depot at Crooklands. Two of the companies very much involved were those of Schneider, Davis & Co., mining at Mouzell, and Town & Rawlinson, with mines at Crossgates. They persuaded the Furness Railway Company to use their powers of compulsory land purchase to help them build tramways from their mines to the ore depot. In March 1849, they were able to announce that a tramway was to be built alongside Butts Beck to the mines at Crossgates. Work began on the Butts tramway the following month, Hunter & Wells being the sub-contractors under Fell & Jopling.

Charles Michael Jopling was a member of that Jopling family who were involved with the Kirkby slate quarries belonging to the Earl of Burlington. John Barraclough Fell had set up in business as a Wharfinger and Timber Merchant at Greenodd in the late 1830s. The two men had already been involved in construction work for the Furness Railway, and were providing horse-drawn omnibuses to run from Dalton station to Ulverston and Newby Bridge. Fell was soon to make his name in partnership with Thomas Brassey, building a mountain railway between Switzerland and Italy over Mont Cenis. Meanwhile, although he unsuccessfully

proposed a narrow-gauge line from Broughton to the copper mines and slate quarries of Coniston, he began the Butts tramway system to the same gauge. This is usually quoted as 3 ft 3½ in, though manufacturers, perhaps a little confused, were also to refer to 3 ft 3 in, 3 ft 4 in, and even, in one instance, 3 ft 3⅜ in. With the fashion for things continental at that time, perhaps the gauge was really intended as one metre.

The tramway was built as a single line, passing under the Ulverston road at Crooklands and then over the Ireleth road on its way up to Crossgates. It was completed by the end of 1849. Operation was by horse power, with some use of gravity to work the downhill trains. This brought its own dangers, and in 1850 the Ulverston Advertiser was reporting that:

> *This line which was opened a short time ago for*
> *the conveyance of ore from the mine of Messrs.*
> *Davis and Co., and Mr. Rawlinson; and which has*
> *proved very beneficial to the town of Dalton, in*
> *regard to cleanliness, in preventing so much of*
> *the ore carting through the east end to Crooklands*
> *station, was the scene of a slight accident, though*
> *not attended with injury to life or limb. The line is*
> *constructed on an incline from the pits to the*
> *station, requiring only the aid of a breaksman in*
> *the descent of the wagons, the empty ones being*
> *drawn back by horses. On Friday morning [22*
> *March] the breaksman descending with a few*
> *wagons was unable to check the speed, and on*
> *their arrival at the station had acquired great*
> *velocity and were thrown off the rails and greatly*
> *damaged; the man in charge escaped unhurt. The*
> *damage done to Mr. Rawlinson's waggons is*
> *estimated upwards of £20.*

The ore from George Ashburner's mines at Elliscales was usually carted down steep roads to Thwaite Flat sidings. This could be a hazardous undertaking, as William Fisher's diary of July 1850 records:

> *Thos Dixon of Dalton met with his death under the following Sircumstances he was carting Iorn ore from Elliscals to wate Flat and in desinding the Steep hill at St Hellins the stays of one of the horses broke and the animal took fright and diseased in is attemp to stop it was thrown backward on the rood and the Cart passed over him nearly severing his head from his body and killing him instantly he was 51 years of age.*

By 1854 the tramway had been extended to Mouzell, and soon after to Elliscales, when the dangers of St Helen's Hill could be set aside. In 1855, Old Hills was connected to the tramway system, and the section from the Crooklands bridge as far as Crossgates was doubled.

The Furness Railway Company's main line from Crooklands had been built as a single line, but pressure from the iron-ore merchants caused the railway company to put in hand the doubling of the line. Lindal tunnel caused particular problems, as the work was to be done without disrupting traffic. Unfortunately, this proved to be impossible when the first length of the new lining collapsed on 5 October 1855. William Fisher's diary carried a report of:

> *2 men working in Lindal Railway Tunnel when a blast exploded Killed one and sadly injured the other so that his life was despaired of.*

The line was out of service for ten days for goods traffic and over two months for passengers. It was not until May 1857 that the contract was eventually completed.

Extensive railway building was being carried out in various parts of the country at this time, and some of these schemes had a considerable effect on life in Furness. The Ulverston(e) & Lancaster opened in 1857, completing the coastal chain of railways and connecting the district with the major railway arteries. Ore traffic for South Staffordshire could now go by rail, and coke from the Wigan coalfield could find its way to Furness. Two years later, the first ironworks opened in Barrow. An experienced engineer was appointed as consultant, Josiah Timmis Smith, who was then working from Windmill Hill, Dudley, and he supervised the erection of three open-topped furnaces, which were provided with high-power blast equipment and inclined-plane loaders. The more modern furnaces such as these used coke for fuel, and operated at a higher temperature than the old bloomeries. With the aid of a flux such as limestone, a liquid alloy of iron and carbon was produced. The limestone, when melted, floated on the surface of the molten iron, so lifting off some of the impurities. After this had been removed, the iron alloy was run off into a mould. The shape of the mould, reminiscent of a sow and her litter, gave the cast iron the name of 'pig iron'. The carbon content was around four per cent, and produced castings that were strong in compression but weak in tension. Further reheating would burn out the carbon to produce wrought iron, strong in tension but weak in compression, and this would then be hammered into rods,

Crooklands, looking across the main lines from near Tantabank. The ore depot can be seen, and an elevated narrow-gauge track is visible.
(Sankey, courtesy Peter Holmes)

Just over a hundred years after the doubling of Lindal tunnel was completed, Class 5 4-6-0 No. 45386 enters with an evening stopping train to Carnforth on 28 June 1958. (Author)

plates or whatever shapes were to be produced. Limestone was found in plenty in Furness, and quarrying was soon established at Goldmire, Greenscoe and Stainton.

The blast furnaces were a mere mile from William Fisher's farmhouse. His diary records:

> The Iron Furnaces was opened at Hindpool Barrow Witnessed by several gentlemen who came by special Train on the 18th October owners Messrs Hannah [Hannay] and Schneider, It was a Galla and beautiful day for the season.

The Ulverston Advertiser had sent along their reporter:

> Tuesday last was quite a gala day at Barrow, in consequence of the opening of the new blast furnaces erected by those spirited capitalists Messrs. Schneider, Hannay & Co., iron ore merchants of this town, and which is looked forward to as the opening of a new era in the history of the iron trade of this district, and is hailed by the people of Barrow as a certain addition to the prosperity of that place.

The after-dinner speeches, *of the most cheering character,* commended the new works as being the *best constructed and most compact in Europe.* In the consultant engineer, Mr Smith, they found *no lack of energy and brains. The Chairman gave The Clergy, coupled with the name of the Rev J M Morgan, vicar of Dalton, which was drunk with much applause.* Responding, *Mr Morgan ... stated that since he came to reside at Dalton there were but one or two* [stationary] *steam engines in Furness, but now he could not hardly go a dozen yards in some localities without seeing one.* Mr Wadham, representing

the Duke of Buccleuch, remarked, *Before the introduction of the railway in Furness, it had been shut out from the rest of the world, isolated and little known, but things had now changed.*

In 1861, the railway was opened between Barnard Castle and Tebay, giving the Barrow works easy access to coke from Durham. To transport the coke was cost-effective for the Furness iron-masters. The Furness ore was rich in iron, with around 60% iron content. This compares with, say, ore from the Cleveland district which had around 30%, making the prices comparable for the end-products.

With the introduction of the Bessemer process for the manufacture of steel, Furness ore came into its own. This process was not able to remove the phosphorus present in most iron ores. The Furness ore was relatively free of phosphorus, and Bessemer himself said that the Furness haematite ore was *indispensible for his purposes.* The steelworks plant at Hindpool was completed in 1865, and this, together with the enlarged ironworks and the Park mines, was purchased by the newly-formed Barrow Haematite Steel Company (BHSC). At a time when wrought iron rails were still widely used on the railways of this country, the plant was primarily set up for the production of steel rails on a large scale, much of which was exported to North America. Barrow was beginning to establish itself as an industrial town of some importance.

The narrow-gauge tramways played their part in helping the iron ore on its way to Barrow. By now there was a comprehensive network of lines, with stretches of double track in places. At Crooklands, the Butts line crossed the main Ulverston road on two levels near the Miner's Arms. There was a bridge under the road to give the main double-track tramway access into the ore yard and onto the stage over the Furness Railway sidings. There was also a level crossing where a third track on a higher level crossed the road to run onto elevated stages used for stockpiling ore along the north-west side of the yard. Steam locomotives were beginning to appear. These generally belonged to BHSC, and they could be found working at other pits under an agreement with the mine owners. Some of these locomotives were of the patent single-cylinder type manufactured by Neilson & Co. of Glasgow. They had a 10-inch cylinder mounted beneath the firebox. They were said to be difficult to handle and erratic in performance, with an inherent tendency to stick on 'dead-centre'.

Improvements to the passenger station at Dalton were very welcome at this time. A plan of 1865 shows the low

main up platform reached from the road up a short flight of steps. The 'station house' had a 'verandah' supported by four columns giving shelter to waiting passengers, and toilets were provided. A goods bay separated from the platform by wooden railings served the goods shed at the western end of the station. For down trains there was an island platform, while behind it sidings fanned out into a yard on the down side of the station. The road still crossed the main running lines by a level crossing, and this had to be used in order to reach the island platform, not an ideal state of affairs. Nevertheless, Daltonians now had a wide variety of destinations which could be reached within a few hours, and all would have been well aware of the daily passage of ore and slate traffic, bearing witness to the growing prosperity of the town and the district.

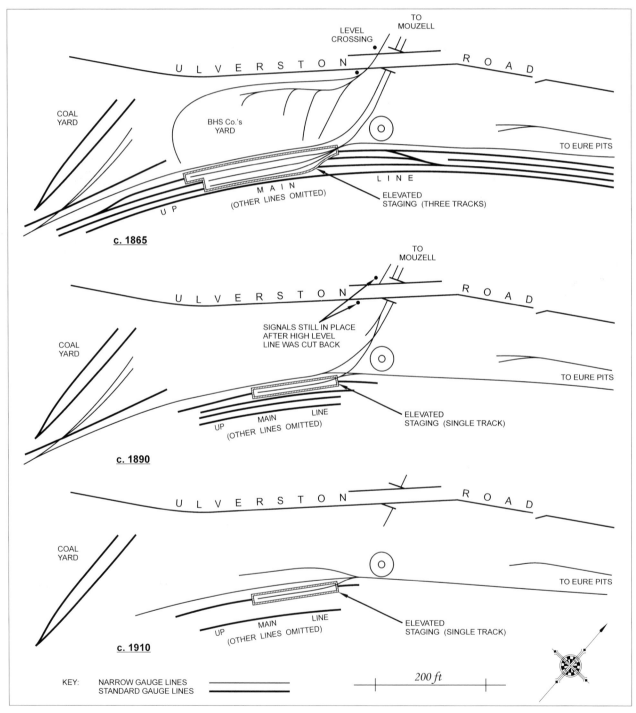

Developments at Crooklands.

(Author / Alan Johnstone)

Mining expansion; the growth of the town; conditions in the mines; the 'Co-op' and other societies; further railway development, train services and railway accidents; the miners' union; further development of the mineral lines; the beginning of the end of the iron industry

Park North Mine as seen from the Askam side.   (Barrow Record Office BDP 37 page 13)

With the opening of the new railway, the bottleneck had been broken. With the line able to handle between 600 and 700 tons of ore a day, there was every incentive for expansion, and large sums of money were spent on mineral exploration in the district. Foremost among these was Henry Schneider, who, with his partner James Davis, was persuaded to take up the mining royalty on land at Park owned by the Earl of Burlington. At first, no serious work was carried out on the site, and it was not until 1850, when the royalty was about to expire and the money available for the work nearly exhausted, that one last effort was made to find ore. Apparently the men offered to work for one more week without pay, a story frequently recounted by Schneider in the years that followed. On this occasion, he did not rely on his Cornish geologists, who had little knowledge of the area, but took local advice, and decided to sink a shaft close to Slater's Farm. At a depth of about 36 feet, a large deposit of ore was discovered. Although it was not known at the time, this was the greatest haematite ore deposit in British history to that date (to be exceeded by the find across the Duddon at Hodbarrow that was made in 1856). It consisted of a continuous mass of ore some 200 yards by 300 yards, containing around

eight and a half million tons of the best quality haematite. The Ulverston Advertiser commented:

> *Messrs. Schneider and Co., whom we stated some time ago, as being sinking for iron ore on the Park Farm, near Dalton, have been so fortunate, we understand (after a diligent and highly praiseworthy effort,) as to find a valuable vein of ore, in close proximity to the Furness Railway. The opening of the vein so far, holds out the most favourable results.*

Having already despatched Cornish beam engines to a number of mines in Mexico, it was not long before Schneider was considering installing one at Park. Evidently intended for the Carlisle Canal Co. but never used, it was put to work in the Park mines in 1856. It had a cylinder diameter of 60 inches, and its horse-power has been estimated at around 150. It had an excellent reputation for reliability. Having described it as *one of the best class*, Richardson, writing in 1880, goes on to say:

> *with the exception of one occasion when it was stopped for 36 hours, it has never suspended working during the 20 years for greater periods than six hours at a time.*

It was to work for 74 years before being eventually replaced by electrical winding equipment.

Other mining companies were also experiencing success, if not on such a grand scale. Joseph Rawlinson was expanding his activities, and in 1853 the Ulverston Advertiser could report that

> Mr Rawlinson, of Dalton, has succeeded in discovering a new vein of iron ore at Carr Kettle, in Pennington, of a quality equal to any in the district, and which bids fair to prove of a very extensive character.

Rawlinson was a local man who lived most of his working life in Dalton. He had quite a range of interests, being lime burner and brick manufacturer as well as ore merchant. But it was his gift for discovering new mineral deposits which earned him his money and gained him his reputation as an astute and successful ironmaster. The discovery of the deposit at Carkettle and the setting up of the Rawlinson Pit in order to mine it was almost certainly the high point of his career. Yet in 1857 he struck lucky again, when he

> found a large deposit of very good quality in Poaka Lots near Martin, in the range of the Lindal Moor vein, of which, no doubt, it is a continuation. This will be a great boon to the neighbourhood. He is now making a railway to the pits, to enable him to get it to the Furness line for shipment.

In 1871 his railway was the scene of some misfortune, as the Barrow Herald explains:

> A serious explosion took place at Mr. Rawlinson's workshops on Tuesday afternoon [7 March] between four and five o'clock, by the bursting of a small locomotive boiler, seriously injuring the driver and a young lad in attendance, both being very much bruised and scalded. Medical attention was promptly got to allay their sufferings. The boiler had just undergone thorough repair at Messrs. Beesley and Sons, boiler makers, Barrow, and had been tested by them to a pressure of 100 lb. per square inch. Just before the accident the locomotive had been run out on the tramway on trial, when a small leakage was discovered about the boom of the boiler. It was then run back into the yard to be examined when the explosion took place, the steam guage (sic) at the time indicating 90 lb. per square inch, with ample water in the boiler and the injector feeding it.

A replacement locomotive was ordered from Fletcher, Jennings of Whitehaven, who supplied another saddle tank of the 0-4-0 wheel arrangement, delivering it the following November.

Rawlinson owned one of the loading piers at Barrow. The excellent quality of the haematite ore mined in Furness was fully recognised by the ironmasters in South Wales and Staffordshire, and there was no difficulty in finding markets.

One such ironmaster was John Brogden, whose family firm in 1850 was developing iron mines in Stainton. Anxious to expedite the transport of the ore to ironworks in South Staffordshire, he had purchased the Ulverston Canal, and was to become a prime mover in the building of the 'Ulverstone and Lancaster Railway'.

The continuing success of the iron ore companies led to increased employment opportunities, and there was a huge influx of labour into the town and into the surrounding villages. Particularly in demand were the experienced miners from Cornwall, who came with their families and settled in the town. Between the censuses of 1851 and 1861, the population of the parish of Dalton approximately doubled, from 4592 in 1851 to 9022 in 1861, and most of this growth was in Dalton township. Rows of terraced houses sprang up, built from the local limestone and the result of a partnership between Joseph Rawlinson, the ironmaster, and James Garden, the builder involved in the construction of Dalton Tunnel.

The hill of High Haume is a familiar landmark outside Dalton, standing in the fork between the roads to Askam and Ireleth. It offers a splendid panoramic view over the town, but the aspect seen today is completely different from what a nineteenth century observer would have seen. John Bolton describes it as he saw it in 1869:

> Before us is the real California of Britain – the great haematite iron ore district of Furness – some of the principal mines forming a semicircle at the base of the hill. Commencing our review at the Northwest, we have first, the new mines of Messrs Kennedy Brothers, on the Askam estate; almost adjoining these the splendid mines of Messrs Schneider, Hannay and Co (this firm has now become the Barrow Haematite Iron and Steel and Mining Co), at Park; close to which are the Roanhead Mines of Kennedy Bros. Glancing round the foot of the hill we find Elliscales, Messrs Ashburner and Son; Butts Beck, Ricket Hills, Cross Gates, J Rawlinson Esq; the Ure Pits, Ulverston Mining Company; Mausell Mines, Messrs Schneider, Hannay and Co; all skirting the base of High Haume, and continuing a circle arc of 180 degrees, with a radius of half a mile.

Today, those out walking their dogs on High Haume must find John Bolton's description difficult to imagine (see map on page 44).

Working conditions in the mines continued to be primitive. Steam was generally only harnessed to power pumping engines; the Brogdens at their mines in Stainton had one of 50 HP that could raise water fifty feet. For men and mineral, however, jackrolls and horse-gins continued. Inevitably there were accidents, with men killed or disabled. The Ulverston Mirror reports one such, in 1869:

> The two men, John Garnett and William Crawford, were being drawn up the shaft in a bucket in the usual manner. When they had proceeded about 40 yards the rope suddenly slipped off the drum at the mouth of the pit, thus causing the bucket containing the men to fall about 20 yards. By the sudden shock Garnett was thrown down the shaft. In the descent his right foot was caught in the wooding of the shaft, and held him suspended head downwards. By a desperate effort he managed to partly raise his body and support himself with one hand, and in this position he remained for about half an hour. As soon as the

ropes were righted he was relieved from his perilous situation and conveyed home. His leg was found to be broken just below the knee and his ankle dislocated and very much crushed. Crawford managed to remain in the bucket, and received some slight damage to his knee.

Even persons of importance were not immune from the dangers. A similar accident occurred to Edward Wadham, who had come into the district in 1854 to be Agent for the Duke of Buccleuch. He had scarcely taken up his post when, descending a shaft at the High Crossgates mine, the bucket was fouled, causing him to fall about twenty feet. He was fortunate to escape with nothing more than a damaged finger.

Working on the surface was no sinecure either, as evidenced by an accident in the rolling mill at Orgrave Ironworks on Friday, 24 November 1848. James Devan, in the act of oiling some machinery, was caught in the spindles with fatal results. The inquest, held at the nearby Black Dog Inn the following day, heard that the accident occurred *for want of proper caution being exercised.* It seems that he, *contrary to the instructions of the overlooker, was oiling the machinery from the wrong side.* James was but fifteen years old, and it seems heartless to modern ears on hearing the proprietors claim that *the deceased had been two years in the mill, and consequently was no stranger to the machinery or its dangers.* Yet at the time it was not uncommon for boys so young to be expected to take on this degree of responsibility, and in doing so they showed a high degree of maturity for their age.

The report in the Ulverston Advertiser lays no blame on the proprietors: after referring to the subscription of over £3 raised by the workforce, they go on to say: *The expenses of the funeral, however, were born by the benevolent proprietors.*

The comradeship that comes with working together in such difficult circumstances, with each man dependent upon his 'mate', led to a close community spirit developing in the town. Evidence of this spirit is the founding of the Dalton-in-Furness Co-operative Society in 1861, one of the earliest in the district. Initially this was to counter the iniquitous practice of the 'tommy shop', company-owned and selling goods at hugely inflated prices, aggravated in some instances by the company paying the men in 'tokens' which could only be 'redeemed' at the company shop. The 'Co-op' returned its profits to the members in the form of a dividend.

The society nearly failed at the first hurdle. A meeting had been called for 11 March in the George and Dragon, near the Parish Church, and the newly-formed Barrow Co-operative Society had been invited to send a delegation. So few people attended that the meeting was adjourned for a week. On its resumption, the Barrow members failed to arrive, and the meeting was about to break up. It was at this point that Thomas Harrison spoke up: 'It is a pity to let it fall through in this way. I am a master and, if you will pay your entrance fees, I will be the responsible man, and will receive all monies, pay all bills, and call all meetings in my name, and will not divulge any person's name.' James Peters stepped forward to pay his entrance fee, others followed, and the society was formed. It was a shaky start, but the fledgling

Dalton Castle, seen from the grounds of the Parish Church. The 'George and Dragon' is on the left of the picture, and part of its signboard can be seen.

(Sankey 2089)

Dalton-in-Furness Co-operative Society's premises in Chapel Street. The offices are on the right beyond the Wesleyan Chapel and above the drapery department. The butcher's shop formed part of the same building. Immediately opposite is the main grocery department, nearer the camera is the men's tailoring department, and just out of shot to the left is the shoe shop. The Co-operative Hall, later to be converted into a cinema, can be seen above the two last-mentioned shops. The entire block was demolished about 1972. (courtesy James Walton)

society was soon on its feet: in the first year of its founding the Dalton society declared a 'divi' of £54; by 1870 it was £2351, and in that year the new Co-operative Hall and Stores, erected by the Dalton contractor, James Garden, were opened. The Park Mines band was in attendance at the opening ceremony, and Henry Schneider remarked that *the working-class of England is the back-bone of the nation.* Complimenting the townspeople on this example of self-help, he went on: *Dalton, the old capital of Furness, has set an example ... to other towns.*

The Bone Club was also started at around the same time. Without National Insurance or the Health and Safety at Work Act, the miners formed this mutual benefit society to provide some financial relief in the event of injury. There was some reassurance in knowing that, if a miner lost a leg and was thereby unable to work, some money would be forthcoming to mitigate the hardship.

On 16 July 1866, the Furness Railway obtained an Act for *the construction of Works, and otherwise in relation to their Undertaking; and for other Purposes.* This 'legalese' included branch lines to Newby Bridge and to the Ulverston Canal. Of interest to Daltonians was the construction of a road bridge to pass over the line at Dalton Station, with the approach road being on a gradient of 1 in 16. Of major importance was a branch line to Stainton. The purpose of this branch was to tap the big limestone deposit which was to be worked to supply the Hindpool blast furnaces. Messrs Benton and Woodiwiss were the contractors. The branch was 1 mile 56 chains long, and accessed from a pair of sidings at Crooklands, situated on the opposite side of the main line from the ore depot. From Crooklands, the line climbed steadily for a little over three quarters of a mile. The gradient

was held to 1 in 50 by constructing the line in an S-curve, swinging left on a quadrant of 10 chains radius followed immediately by another quadrant of 14 chains radius to the right. Milepost 24 (miles from Carnforth) was situated near the top of the incline. The line continued on the level for almost a mile to Stainton, where it served the limestone quarries as well as the iron mines operated by the Brogden company on land belonging to the Earl of Derby. It was ready for use in 1868, and on 5 February the first load of limestone was on its way to Hindpool. 65,000 tons of limestone were moved in the first year of operation.

Another boost to Dalton's importance came with the opening of the 'expedition curve' connecting Goldmire Junction with Dalton Junction. This 'Millwood Curve' had been opened in 1858. At first it saw sporadic use by passenger trains (the morning Coniston-Carnforth soon after the Coniston Railway opened, for example), and it was mainly used for goods traffic. It was the scene of an accident on 11 November 1870. The boat from Belfast having docked late at Piel, a special train was put on for its passengers, leaving at 10.30 a.m. After calling at Furness Abbey, the train continued towards Dalton. At Dalton Junction, a mineral train was being allowed out from the 'expedition curve' in front of the special. Ignoring the signals until it was too late, the driver of the special ran into the mineral train at the junction, damaging his engine and derailing some of the wagons. There were only two passengers on the special, both in the last coach, and they sustained no serious injury. The Ulverston Advertiser wrote sympathetically of the engine driver of the special: *He is a man who has borne an excellent character for steadiness and care.* Lieutenant-Colonel Rich, in his report to the Board of Trade, was rather more

Crooklands in the mid-1930s, looking towards Dalton station. The Stainton branch climbs away to the left. What remained of Crooklands signal box is in the centre of the picture (the box closed on 1 December 1935).   *(CRA Pattinson collection PA0075)*

critical of the driver, writing: *The accident was caused solely by his want of caution.* The hapless driver had been seventeen years in the Company's service, nine of them as a driver. Col. Rich had some hard words to say about the signalling, that *the line from Dalton Junction to Furness Abbey is signalled in a very indifferent manner.* Nor did he see much virtue in the new locking frame in course of erection at Dalton Junction, describing the system as *decidedly objectionable.*

The down mail train made its appearance in the timetable from 1 September 1869. Leaving Carnforth at 4.30 a.m., this train made calls at Grange and Ulverston. It then traversed the Millwood Curve to reach Foxfield Junction

(as it was then known) at 5.40 a.m. before continuing up the coast to Whitehaven. However, from 1 July 1871, it was retimed to leave Carnforth at 4 a.m., and then made an additional stop at Dalton to make a connection with a Barrow train. The mail train also conveyed passengers travelling overnight from London (Euston), and on the morning of 22 May 1872 some of those passengers had a rude awakening. The connecting train from Barrow and Furness Abbey was usually shunted across to the far side of the island platform before the mail train arrived. On this morning however, it had been delayed at a level crossing; the gates were closed against the railway *contrary to the*

Stainton Quarry, with railway lines leading towards the quarry face. (Sankey, courtesy Jeffrey Sankey)

29

Act of Parliament and the gatekeeper was in bed. As a result, the shunting had not been completed when the mail train arrived. In the collision, two of the carriages of the Barrow train were derailed, but the mail train stayed on the track, with only slight damage to the engine, the front van and the following carriage. No-one sustained injury except for the guard of the mail train who received slight bruising when he was knocked against the partition of his van.

Lieutenant-Colonel Rich again conducted the enquiry for the Board of Trade. He found that, while the signal box at Crooklands was closed at night and the signals left at 'clear', the Dalton station box was operating and the signals had been correctly set at danger against the down mail. The driver of the mail train agreed that this was so, but he excused himself by saying, that he never contemplated any danger when he saw the Dalton station signal "up" against his train. He was in the habit of running into the station daily with the signal at danger against him. Col. Rich was emphatic: *The company's rule book is plain and distinct...but...the practice is quite different to the rule, and...it...is not surprising that accidents should happen under such circumstances.* He concluded, *The men appeared to be good men, and they have no doubt done their duties as seemed best to them, but the supervision seems to have been very lax.*

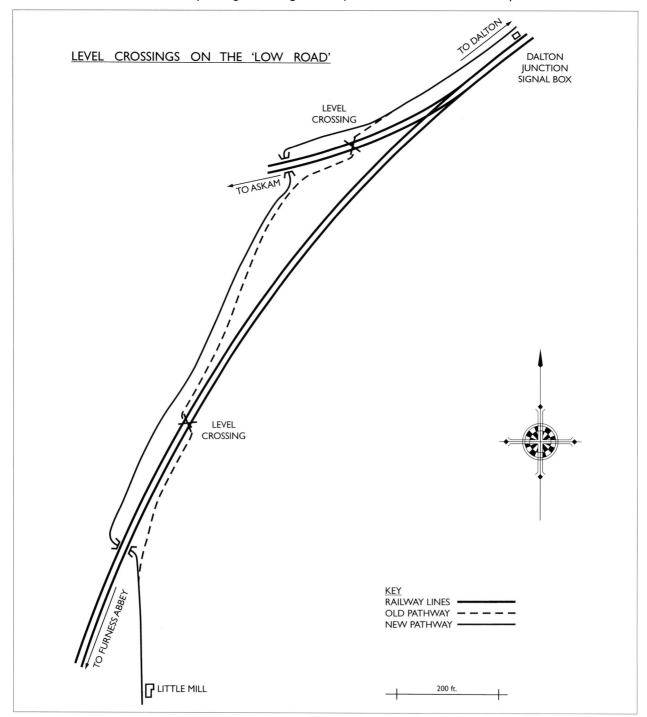

LEVEL CROSSINGS ON THE 'LOW ROAD'

TO DALTON

DALTON JUNCTION SIGNAL BOX

LEVEL CROSSING

TO ASKAM

LEVEL CROSSING

KEY
RAILWAY LINES
OLD PATHWAY
NEW PATHWAY

TO FURNESS ABBEY

LITTLE MILL

200 ft.

The Furness Railway was finding the large number of level crossings on the line an increasing embarrassment. A section in the 1866 Act authorised the replacement of a number of these crossings with bridges, though the work proceeded very slowly. The map shows the route of the 'Low Road' with its two level crossings, together with the modifications needed when the underpasses were built. This work was completed in 1884.

(Author / Alan Johnstone, from Barrow Record Office Plan Ref. 115)

STATIONS.	37 Coke.	38 Coke and Empties.	39 Roose Ore?	40 Ore and Emptys	41 Bank Engine and Coke.	42	43 Park Empties	44 Passenger	45 Thro Goods and M'lom Coke
	p.m.	p.m.	p.m.	p.m.	p.m.	p.m.	p.m.	p.m.	p·m.
Midland ....arrive	10 30							1 5	
L.N.W. ....arrive	11 0	12 30						1 10	
Carnforth ......depart	12 10	1 10						1 30	
" ..F. & M. Junc.								1 35	
Silverdale									
Arnside									
Meathop....................									
Grange								1 50	
Kents Bank									
Cark									
Levens Viaduct	1 20	2 s 0							
Ulverston ...... arrive								2 8 (s)	
Windermere Branch — Ulverston ..depart								2 15	
Greenodd								2 21	
Haverthwaite								2 27	
Lake Side .. arrive								2 40	
Lake Side ..depart								1 35	
Haverthwaite								1 42	
Greenodd								1 50	
Ulverston								2 0	
Ulverston								2 10	
Lindal	2 s 50	2 30			2 45			s	3 30
Crooklands	3 0								
Dalton	3 10							2 20	
Park					3 0				3 45
Barrow Branch — Furness Abbey........								2 25	
Roose									
Piel									
Barrow..................	3 30							2 40	
Hindpool .... arrive	3 40								
Hindpool ....depart							2 20		
Barrow..................				1 0			2 40	2 0	2 40
Piel									
Roose				1 30				2 5	
Furness Abbey....								2 10	
Dalton								2 23	
Park				1 50			3 0		4 0
Askam Iron Works......				2 20					4 10
Askam					3 10			2 32	4 20
Dunnerholme									
Kirkby								2 40	4 30
Foxfield Junction......								2 46	4 50
Coniston Branch — Broughton								2 55	
Woodland								3 2	
Torver								3 10	
Coniston...... arrive								3 20	
Coniston......depart								12 45	
Torver								12 52	
Woodland								1 0	
Broughton..........								2 35	
Foxfield								2 50	5 10
Greenroad..............									
Underhill									
Millom				5 0				3 s 0	5 s 50
Silecroft..................									
Bootle....................								3 15	
Eskmeals									
Ravenglass								3 25	
Drigg								3 30	
Seascale								3 35	
Sellafield Junction......				6 s 35				3 40	7 0
Braystones............									
Nethertown									
St. Bees								3 s 55	
Corkickle				7 10				4 5	7 25
Whitehaven .... arrive				7 15				4 10	7 30

(Column 38 in the lower Barrow Branch section is marked "When required.")

No. 37 Down Goods to shunt for 44 Down Pass. at Lindal
No. 38 Down Goods to shunt at Levens for 44 Down Passenger.
No. 40 Down Goods to cross 75 Up Passenger at Sellafield.
No. 44 Down Passenger to pass 38 Down Goods at Levens, 37 Down Goods at Lindal, and 35 Down Goods at Millom and cross 66 Up Pass. at St. Bees.

An extract from the 1877 Working Timetable, during the period when Dalton was the interchange point for through trains between Carnforth and Whitehaven and trains for the 'Barrow Branch'. The 1.30 p.m. departure from Carnforth is booked to stand at Dalton from 2.20 p.m. to 2.23 p.m. for the benefit of passengers travelling to or from Barrow. (Cumbrian Railways Association)

These 2-4-0 locomotives built by Sharp, Stewart & Co. handled much of the passenger traffic through Dalton. (Mike Peascod collection)

On the introduction of the summer timetable on 1 May 1873 it became general for through passenger trains between Whitehaven and Carnforth to use the 'Millwood Curve'. Then Dalton took over from Furness Abbey the handling of the exchange traffic. This must have reduced the travelling time for passengers making through journeys between north and south, but it was rather less than convenient for passengers for Barrow. The arrangement continued for nearly ten years, until the opening of the Barrow and Park loop lines on 1 June 1882. The timetable suggests some smart working would have been necessary if the timetable was to be adhered to and delays avoided.

Hopefully, too, the supervision commented upon unfavourably by Col. Rich had been improved. However, the risk of an accident is never far away, as this account of an *exciting scene* at Dalton station on Christmas Eve, 1881, reported in the Barrow Herald, shows:

> *Persons accustomed to travel on the Furness Railway will know that when a train arrives at Dalton from Barrow it rushes through the station and then shunts the carriages back again towards the furthest platform. On Saturday evening the train had gone through the station and most of the passengers for Barrow and Whitehaven way had crossed over the line and as soon as the engine was returning to get on the front of the return train to Barrow, two men ran across the line, one of whom, in attempting to spring upon the platform, fell flat upon his back across the*

> *metals. The driver seeing the circumstances, instantly reversed his engine and it was brought to a standstill within three yards of the man.*

The passenger traffic was in the hands of 2-4-0 locomotives attached to four-wheeled tenders. The company had nineteen of these little engines, built by Sharp, Stewart & Co., which were the mainstay of the services until 1890. During the summer months, train loads could be as many as ten or twelve coaches, both four-wheelers and six-wheelers.

Barrow had become sufficiently important to become a borough in 1867, with a population of around 15,000. This coincided with the walling up of the Barrow Channel and its conversion into the two great dock basins, Devonshire (opened that year) and Buccleuch (completed in 1873). Dalton was sufficiently anxious as to seek its own local board, to prevent the possible absorption of the town into the new Borough of Barrow, and to avoid any consequent increase in rates. This authority came into being in 1873. A leading member was William Crossley, manager of the Furness Iron & Steel Company, the proprietors of the newly established Askam Ironworks and to whom Joseph Rawlinson sold off his mining interests before retiring to Ulverston. The Local Board improved the roads in the district and made a determined effort to tackle the sewerage problems in the town. This was done without significantly raising the district rate, the increased rating of the ore mines absorbing the costs. The market, earlier revitalised with the huge increase in the population of the town, was once again on the decline, being unable to compete with the covered facilities offered by its neighbours in Ulverston and Barrow. A market hall was proposed, on a site in Station Road, but in the event it was offices and a fire station that were built. The police station, erected in Market Street towards the close of the century, was built in a similar style. The limestone stonework set off with sandstone quoins presented a very elegant appearance.

The expansion of the iron and steel works at Hindpool, together with the substantial new dockyards being erected, saw a sharp increase in Barrow's population. James Ramsden had been the railway's first Locomotive Superintendent and was now its General Manager. As Barrow's Mayor, he had a vision for the town, and was beginning to see it realised. The Furness Railway Act 1872, which had received its Royal Assent on 18 July of that year, authorised a number of new railway lines, including the 'Barrow Loop Line', with a new 'Barrow Central' station in Abbey Road. A trade depression caused the work to be held up, but on 1 June 1882 the new line was opened. Traffic was routed through the new station in Barrow, and no more was Dalton to be the 'Crewe Junction' of Furness.

There were few complaints from through passengers about the extra journey time, so perhaps the train working at Dalton had not been very 'smart' after all. It was also a boon to Barrow residents, but for local passengers travelling from Millom and Askam to Dalton or Ulverston, it made the journey some seven miles longer. This aroused the ire of the Ulverston Mirror, whose Editorial of 10 June 1882 read:

> *The alterations that have recently been made by the Furness Railway Company constitute, so far as this town [Ulverston] and Furness at large, with the sole exception of Barrow itself, are concerned, one of the most high-handed, audacious and monstrous schemes ever devised by an ambitious and overreaching town to damage a whole district for the express purpose of benefiting itself. Dalton, which used to be reached by the 7.50 a.m. from Coniston at 8.55 is now reached at 9.11 a.m.*

These were strong words indeed, and when the Local Boards of Ulverston, Dalton and Millom threatened to complain to the Board of Trade, the Furness Railway backed down. From July they provided a 9.25 a.m. from Millom to Ulverston via the Dalton Loop, returning from Dalton (with a connection from Ulverston) at 3.59 p.m. by the same route. There were several attempts to take off these 'Local Board trains' because of poor patronage, but they continued in a scaled-down form until the Great War. In 1908 there was only the one train, leaving Askam for Dalton at 9.33 a.m. and with no return working.

The railway accident for which the Furness company is best known occurred at Lindal Ore Sidings on the morning of 22 September 1892, when a series of subsidences succeeded in entombing 'Sharpie' goods locomotive No. 115. This was fortunately without serious injury to anyone, though Driver Postlethwaite was somewhat upset to lose his jacket and gold watch along with his engine. Daltonians must have been affected by the disruption to traffic, which was not back to normal until the following Spring.

In 1898, the 'Local Board train' was involved in an incident at Dalton station which could have had serious consequences but for the prompt action of the railway staff. On Thursday morning, 16 June, the train had arrived in the station with passengers looking forward to a day at the

Market Street from Tudor Square. The Police Station is prominent.

(Sankey 4741)

Dalton station from Greystone Mount. The main station building, the canopies and the covered stairs to the road bridge can be seen. At this date the independent covered way had yet to be added. (courtesy James Walton)

Dalton-in-Furness

V. & S., D.

Ulverston Market. The locomotive uncoupled, ready to collect two horse-boxes standing in the cattle siding. A heavy mineral train was waiting at Crooklands. A coupling chain broke, allowing loaded ore wagons to break away from their train and run back towards the station *at a terrific pace.* Swift action by Driver Stackhouse, who promptly ran his engine out of the siding, and by Signalman Sandham, who just as quickly switched the points, was sufficient to avert a collision. The stationmaster (Mr Crookhall) and a porter (Mr Kitchin) helped bring the wagons to a halt by applying the wagon brakes as they trundled by. The Ulverston Advertiser records that the *incident created the greatest excitement among the passengers on the train as well as the large crowd on the platform.* The excitement was too much for the fireman, who jumped off, *but the engine driver stuck boldly to his post.* Signalman Sandham received an honorarium of twenty shillings and a letter of commendation for the *promptness and foresight* he had displayed.

In due course the station was enlarged and improved, largely in the form in which it remained until taken into British Rail ownership. The old up platform was raised and new offices erected, which included a wood-panelled booking hall. Passengers had the protection of ornate cast iron canopies, the Furness Railway company's monogram being incorporated into the scrollwork. On the down side the island platform served two roads, the trackwork and signalling allowing trains to leave from platform 3 in either direction. A wood and glass canopy with end screens was provided, though this was later replaced by a plainer structure of steel. There were goods sidings on both sides of the line, the principal yard being on the south side, where coal and cattle wharves served the needs of the local traders. Access to the platforms was provided from the overbridge on the Stainton road. Platforms and offices were lit by gas, supplied by the town's own gasworks at Goose Green.

The railway timetable also began to assume the shape it was to maintain throughout the Grouping and into the Nationalisation years. The crack train of the day was the lunchtime express to London. It was introduced in 1878.

The Ulverston Advertiser commended this *great boon to travellers* when it began running on 1 July, *leaving Barrow at one o'clock in the afternoon, Ulverston 1-25, reaching London at eight o'clock in the evening, running the whole distance in seven hours.* There was a connection with the train leaving Whitehaven at 11.30 a.m. In January, 1886, this train reached Carnforth just 46 minutes after leaving Dalton, with station stops at Ulverston and Grange, but before long it ceased to call at Dalton or Grange, an earlier stopping service being provided for intermediate passengers. The morning down mail train from Carnforth, with stops at Grange and Ulverston, needed about forty minutes before arrival at Dalton some time after 5 a.m., while in the reverse direction the up night mail left Dalton some time after 9 p.m. with a very similar schedule. The Furness line enjoyed through coaches to a variety of destinations: the London & North Western Railway gave access to London (Euston), Liverpool and Manchester, and the Midland Railway ran to London (St Pancras), Sheffield, Leeds and Bradford. By now, William Pettigrew had been appointed as Locomotive Superintendent, and larger locomotives of the 4-4-0 wheel arrangement were in use on the fastest and heaviest trains. To cater for passengers travelling to intermediate stations without unduly delaying the train, a method of 'slip working' was popular. The guard detached the 'slip' coach while the train was approaching the station. The train then continued through the station without stopping, the guard bringing the 'slip' coach to a halt in the platform under the action of its own brakes. At one time the Furness Railway was operating no fewer than seven such 'slips'. In 1891 Dalton had one, detached from the 10.05 a.m. Barrow-Lakeside, but it was short-lived.

Local government reorganisation saw the conversion of the old Local Board into a Town Council (UDC) at the beginning of 1895. Its members were drawn from a good cross-section of the population of the town, for beside James Brocklebank, gentleman, we find James Butcher, engine driver, and William Lewney, miner. Level crossings were an ever-present problem. A man was injured at Thwaite Flat crossing,

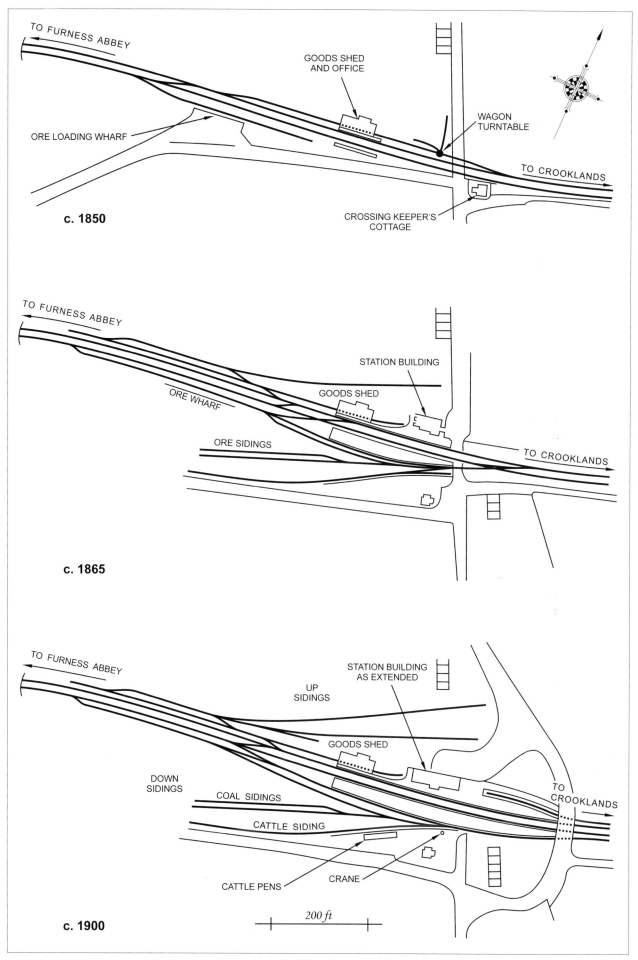

TO FURNESS ABBEY

GOODS SHED
AND OFFICE

WAGON
TURNTABLE

ORE LOADING WHARF

TO CROOKLANDS

c. 1850

CROSSING KEEPER'S
COTTAGE

TO FURNESS ABBEY

STATION BUILDING

GOODS SHED

ORE WHARF

ORE SIDINGS

TO CROOKLANDS

c. 1865

TO FURNESS ABBEY

STATION BUILDING
AS EXTENDED

UP
SIDINGS

GOODS SHED

DOWN
SIDINGS

TO
CROOKLANDS

COAL SIDINGS

CATTLE SIDING

CRANE

CATTLE PENS

200 ft

c. 1900

Developments at Dalton Station.

(Author / Alan Johnstone)

resulting in both legs being amputated. He had been unable to see the approaching train because of the presence of the signal box (Park South). The councillors, discussing this at their meetings in 1900, said they had been unable to persuade the platelayer to open the locked gates without instructions from Barrow. The situation was made the more difficult in that, since the creation of the Barrow Borough, one gate was in Barrow and the other in Dalton. The railway company was pressed to install a bridge at the location, but to no avail.

Train movements in and around the station could still provide the excitement of the day. The Barrow News records one such incident:

> At 11 a.m. on Monday [11 August 1913] a singular mishap, happily unattended by any serious consequences, occurred at the Dalton railway station. Shunting operations were proceeding, and the engine-driver was under the impression that he was going on the main line, instead of which the train was turned into the siding, coming into violent contact with the stop-block. The result of the impact was that two coaches and two compartments of another coach were derailed, and the windows of several other carriages broken. No personal injuries were sustained. Services of the breakdown gang were secured by the stationmaster (Mr G. Stephenson), and by two o'clock the damaged coaches were removed.

It needed smart work indeed to have the whole scene cleared in around three hours, but this was not quick enough to avoid the attentions of a few Dalton youngsters and even a local photographer.

It was no easy task to form a trade union for miners. Nevertheless, the Furness Miners and Quarrymen's Union was inaugurated on 22 December 1888. John Myers was appointed secretary. He had been educated at the Green School, Dalton, and had served his time as a shoemaker before going to work underground at Park Mine. He was an able secretary, and needed to use all his skills on more than one occasion. The unwillingness of the employers to recognise a union and its officers is well illustrated by the problems that arose at Roanhead mines in the early months of 1900. The miners sought an increase in pay and an adjustment in the hours of labour. Messrs Kennedy, it was reported, *have steadily refused to conduct negotiations with the general secretary of the Miners' Association.* When a strike was called, Myles Kennedy said he was willing to meet his miners, but insisted there should be present *no outside party.* A mass meeting in a field near Park Farm showed feelings running high. A few miners continued to work, and they had to be escorted home by police, running the gauntlet of a daily demonstration. The Ulverston Advertiser reported a potentially ugly scene while such a demonstration was taking place:

> on Friday morning [25 May] *when one of the 'blacklegs' was returning to his home in Cleator-street, seven policemen – Sergts. McDonald and Moore with five constables – had to be requisitioned to control the crowd of two thousand people and escort the men home through Chapel-street, which was lined with people shouting and hooting.*

The ranks of strikers thinned as they found other work, but, with no sign of a settlement, it was decided to send a

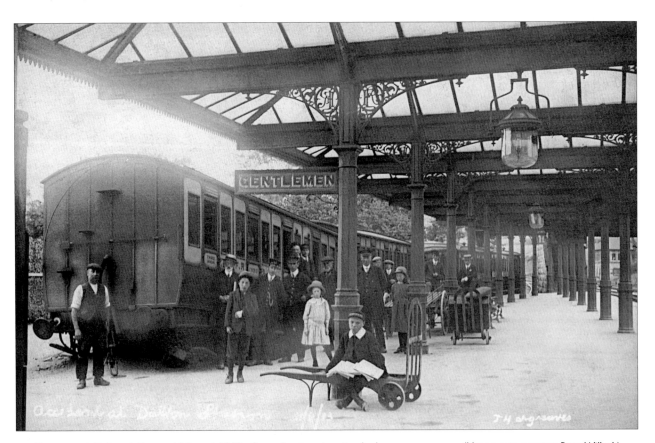

The scene at Dalton station on 11 August 1913, after a shunting operation had gone wrong.   (Hargreaves, courtesy Peter Willock)

deputation of six miners accompanied by Mr Myers. Eventually, in the middle of July, the strike was settled to the men's satisfaction, with a pay award of from 6s 4d to 6s 6d per day and a change of hours implemented on the basis of a three-months' trial.

Shortly afterwards, the miners at Roanhead hit the headlines again, but for an entirely different reason. The Ulverston Advertiser reported:

> A somewhat remarkable "find" in one of the workings at Rita Pit, Roanhead Mines, was reported on Saturday [22 September]. A solid piece of kidney ore [pure haematite], and estimated at 2 tons weight, was struck, and a party of 15 miners were allotted the task of removing it whole to the surface. The task was successfully carried out on Saturday evening. Never before has such a huge piece of solid ore been raised at any one mine in the district, and it is confidently stated that "the find" proves conclusively that the Roanhead Mines are still very rich in metal.

It had been cut free from the surrounding ore without the use of dynamite in order to avoid damage. When the time came to raise it, it was found to be too large for the cage. Parts of the shaft timbers had to be cut away before the cage, the precious ore slung underneath and held by chains, was lifted slowly to the surface. By all accounts, people came from far and near to see it on display in the Roanhead wagon shop.

Mr Myers gave up the post of secretary in 1904, and became a school attendance officer. He was prominent in the affairs of the town, being a member of the Dalton Board, subsequently becoming a Councillor, a member of the School Board and also on the Dalton Co-operative Society Committee. He was a staunch and active Congregationalist, was involved in the Dalton Liberal Club, enjoyed a game of bowls at Dalton Cricket Club, and was a gifted poet in the local Dalton dialect.

Mr Myers was succeeded as secretary of the union by Mr Lewney. William Lewney was an 'off-comer' to the town, whose father Robert, in search of work, had brought the family over from the Isle of Man in 1879. William was among those who helped to form the Furness Miners and Quarrymen's Union. *Level-headed, practical and eminently fair*, he became a much respected member of the community. He was to hold the office of President of the Co-operative Society for fifteen years. By 1905 he had become chairman of Dalton Urban District Council, as well as general secretary of his union. This was a critical time for the mining industry, for while Henry Schneider's company operated a sliding scale, which guaranteed each miner a minimum wage of six shillings a day, the Harrison, Ainslie company did not. The Barrow Herald reported that:

> there is every possibility of a strike taking place at the Lindal Moor mines this weekend. Mr W Lewney, Secretary of the Dalton & District Workmen's Association, declines to give any information on the subject; but we understand that unless the management give way the whole of the miners will cease work on Saturday next.

Mr Lewney.   (Barrow Record Office BDP 72)

> The point in dispute is that up to the present the sliding scale, which is in operation at Park and Roanhead Mines, has not been adopted at Lindal Moor. At a meeting of the men held recently, it was decided that unless their employers acceded to their request by Saturday, December the 16th, they would come out on strike. The contention of the managers is that seeing the operations at their mines are mostly of a speculative character the sliding scale could not be applied with satisfactory results.

The mines manager was Mr Charles Ray of Whinfield House, Lindal. His willingness to talk to the press was in marked contrast with his reluctance to negotiate with Mr Lewney. There was a mass meeting of the entire membership of the union in Dalton, at which Mr Lewney gave a full account of the situation. The members gave the Lindal Moor men their full support, resolving to raise a levy if financial assistance became necessary. The management reacted by sacking the entire workforce two days before Christmas. This tamed many of the men, and brought many unemployed flocking to Lindal to fill up the ranks. Some of these were out-of-work slate quarrymen from Coniston. Interestingly, no instances of intimidation against these 'blacklegs' were reported in the local press, unlike the earlier strike at Roanhead, and even more unlike the contemporaneous strike of blacksmiths in the Barrow shipyard, by all accounts a dirty and bloody affair in comparison.

In 1910 Mr Lewney was appointed to sit on a Royal Commission on Metalliferous Mines and Quarries, the only British miner to do so. He died in 1922, shortly after declining an offer of an OBE for his services during the

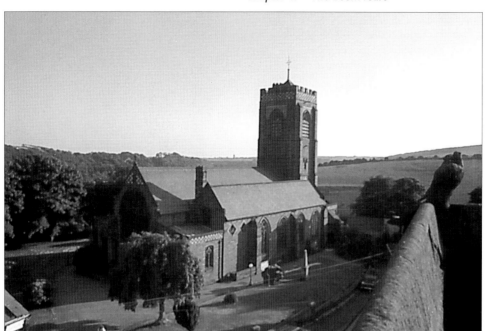

Dalton Parish Church, seen from the castle battlements.
(Alan Johnstone)

Great War. On the day of his funeral, the Dalton Co-operative Society closed its shops and offices for the day, and his coffin was carried by some of those iron miners he had represented for the greater part of his life.

In 1883, the Parish Church was in extensive need of repair and renovation. Sir James Ramsden - he had been knighted in 1872 - was a member of the Building Committee present at the inaugural meeting to discuss its rebuilding. The noted Lancaster firm of architects, Paley and Austin, was chosen to design what was effectively a new building. The contractor for the work was the Dalton builder, James

Garden. The vicar of Dalton, the Revd James Morrison (Paddy) Morgan, graduate of St Bees College, was a capable man and a good organiser, but not one to suffer fools. When Garden quoted £70 for some additional item for the church, the vicar commented that it would have been £17 if done by anyone else. But the gentry and the business interests contributed handsomely for this noble cause: the Duke of Devonshire and the Duke of Buccleuch, the Barrow Haematite Steel Company, Henry Schneider, the Kennedy brothers, Harrison, Ainslie & Company all figure prominently, together with others. Particularly notable was the

Photographed from the Ruskinville bridge, Class 47 No. 47 542 passes Dalton Junction signal box with the 1105 Barrow-Preston on 7 April 1982. The skylight on the signal box roof can be seen, and the tall signals controlling the junction. *(Author)*

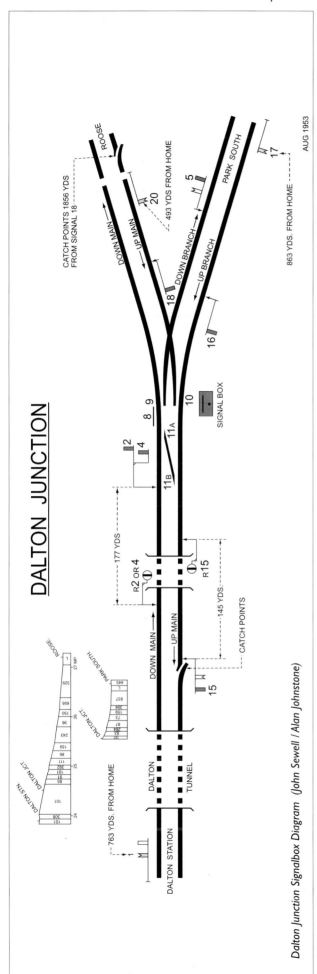

DALTON JUNCTION

ROOSE

CATCH POINTS 1856 YDS
FROM SIGNAL 18

DOWN MAIN

UP MAIN

20

493 YDS FROM HOME

5

DOWN BRANCH

UP BRANCH

PARK SOUTH

17

863 YDS. FROM HOME

AUG 1953

18

16

8 9

SIGNAL BOX

10

2

4

11A

11B

177 YDS

R2 OR 4

R15

145 YDS.

CATCH POINTS

DOWN MAIN

UP MAIN

15

ROOSE

PARK SOUTH.

DALTON JCT.

DALTON JCT.

DALTON STN.

DALTON

TUNNEL

763 YDS. FROM HOME

DALTON STATION

Dalton Junction Signalbox Diagram (John Sewell / Alan Johnstone)

*The signals at the junction were originally even taller.
(CRA Pattinson collection PA 0081)*

contribution of the Duke of Devonshire. He not only contributed the substantial sum of £3,500, but also paid for the East Window which he gave in memory of his second son, Lord Frederick Cavendish. Lord Frederick had been assassinated in Phoenix Park, Dublin in May 1882, where he had gone to take up his post as Chief Secretary for Ireland. The new church was consecrated on 1 June 1885 by the Rt Revd Harvey Goodwin, Bishop of Carlisle.

On 12 June 1889, an accident took place in Ireland that was to have a profound effect on Britain's railways. A collision at Armagh on a steep gradient occurred, between a passenger train and an excursion train full of schoolchildren, and it caused greater loss of life than any other accident which had occurred on Britain's railways up to that time. The line was worked, not on the absolute block (space) system, but by time interval. The report on the accident asserted that *if the block telegraph system had been in force . . . the results of this collision would have been considerably mitigated.* Public opinion was aroused, and, before the year was out, the 'Regulation of Railways Act 1889' made block working and interlocking of points and signals compulsory.

As a result of this Act, the Furness Railway began an extensive programme of improvements to their signalling system. Some main-line boxes were replaced, some of them seeing service in a lesser capacity on branch lines. Three signal boxes looked after the traffic in the Dalton area. Crooklands box, situated in the fork between the main down line and the Stainton branch, had a 22-lever frame to control the complex of lines in that vicinity.

Hunslet locomotive Greenscoe, *with the Twiname brothers on the footplate.*   (Barrow Record Office BDP 16)

Dalton Station box was also on the down side of the tracks, just north of the road overbridge. Similar in appearance to the boxes at Park South and at St Bees, it had a 30-lever frame, and looked after the lines in the immediate environs of the station. Dalton Junction box controlled the divergence of the 'loop line' to Park from the main line to Barrow, and still exercises that function today. The present box was built in 1902, with a 20-lever frame. The signals which controlled the junction were very tall, to give engine drivers a view of them over the Ruskinville bridge. So that the signalman could see them without performing contortions, a skylight was incorporated into the roof of the box, and this was only removed on renovation of the box in 1987 after colour-light signals had been installed at this location.

When the Askam & Mouzell Iron Co. Ltd. acquired the ironworks at Askam, they were anxious to link their adjacent mining and iron smelting activities, while at the same time avoiding the obligation to use the Furness Railway to transport their ore. They built a standard-gauge line from the Mouzell mines to Askam, which opened in August, 1882. The use of the Furness Railway Directors' Saloon, borrowed for the occasion and hauled by an ironworks locomotive, suggests that the Furness Railway was not too upset by the loss of traffic. The Mouzell branch became a well-known sight alongside the Dalton to Askam road, which it crossed in three places, and these bridges became something of a nuisance when motor traffic became common along the road.

It was obviously convenient, to enable through running, for the narrow-gauge tramways running from Mouzell and Elliscales to be replaced by standard gauge, and this conversion was carried out as far as Crossgates, the line down to Crooklands remaining narrow gauge. Most of the ore was now destined for ironworks at Askam or Millom,

and the initial start from Crossgates in that direction was up a very steep gradient of around 1 in 15. The curvature of the track formation compounded the difficulty. There was a shunting loco shedded at Mouzell to collect the full iron ore wagons. From 1895, a 14-inch four-coupled Peckett locomotive undertook this task, replacing a similar but larger six-coupled machine which had been found to be too big. A locomotive from the ironworks would come up at least once a day with the empty wagons. This was a 15-inch six-coupled Hunslet of 1876, named *Greenscoe*. The two engines would then take the full wagons up the grade four at a time; the noise of the Peckett and *Greenscoe* roaring and slipping up to the farm crossing could be heard all over Dalton. The driver of the Peckett was Jack Twiname, while his elder brother Bill drove *Greenscoe*. Bill had only one hand, and was well-known for his habit of throwing coal from his moving engine at any children who happened to stray within throwing distance. Despite this, Bill was a popular character, and, when times were hard, he would often roll a large lump of coal off the loco for the people at Green Haume farm.

Other mines had their rail systems, notably those at Park, where sidings were built beside the Furness Railway, a network of standard-gauge tramways connecting them to all the pits of the Park mines. BHSC locomotives operated here, that company having a fleet of 0-4-0 saddle-tank locomotives. Some were built by Neilson, of its patent single-cylinder type, similar to the narrow-gauge engines supplied to the Butts tramway. Others were built by Sharp, Stewart, and these included six locomotives acquired from the Furness Railway. The six were a development of the earlier 'Coppernob' locomotives, and were only some seven years old when they were purchased, without tenders, from that company. They were rebuilt as saddle-tanks, and at least two of these engines worked at Park over a long period of time.

Park Mines, with an 0-4-0 locomotive, almost certainly a rebuilt 'Neilson', at work.   (Barrow Record Office BDP 37 page 8)

A sketch of a Neilson single-cylinder 0-4-0 saddle-tank locomotive.   (Peter Holmes)

Park Mines, with one of the former Furness Railway 0-4-0 engines rebuilt as a saddle tank locomotive.

(Barrow Record Office BDP 37 page 4)

Also forming a junction with the Furness Railway at Park was the rail system of the Kennedy family's Roanhead mines. This covered a greater distance between Park and the seashore, a maze of lines which wound between the areas of broken ground. Near Kathleen Pit, two lines ran northwards to converge near 'The Lots', and connected with the main line using the Askam Ironworks siding. Ore for Askam or Millom was despatched by this 'North Line' rather than using Park Sidings. One of the locomotives working at Roanhead was an 0-6-0 saddle tank named *M.T.B.K.* This was named for one of the Kennedy brothers, Myles Theodore Burton Kennedy. As the driver was a Mr Molyneaux, this inevitably became 'Moly's Tin Brass Kettle'. Andrew Barclay supplied two further 0-6-0s, *Wilfrid* in 1911 and *Roanhead* in 1915, and these locomotives worked the traffic until the mines closed.

There was another narrow-gauge tramway at Crooklands, built in 1862 to the Eure Pits and then on to High Crossgates, to serve the mines and quarries of the Brogden family. Known as 'The Lindal Moor narrow gauge', this line was initially worked by horses until about 1872, when John Brogden & Co. took delivery of an 0-4-0 saddle tank locomotive from Black Hawthorn & Co. of Gateshead. The tramway was used by Barrow contractor Coulton Walker Hunter for a time, to move limestone from Eure Pits quarry down to Crooklands. He used a vertical-boilered

'Coffeepot' locomotive bought new from Balmforth Brothers Ltd., of Rodley in Yorkshire; the locomotive chimney was hinged to enable it to pass through the tunnel under the Urswick road. There were the inevitable mishaps when the driver, perhaps the worse for drink, forgot to actuate the hinge. When the quarry closed in 1909, the locomotive moved to Millwood, where it was used in the construction of the earthworks for the road improvements there.

In the 1870s competition arrived in the shape of cheap iron ore imported from Spain. Low wages and the poor living conditions allowed to the Spanish miners helped to market their ore so cheaply. At the same time, some export markets were disappearing as countries developed their own resources; in North America, for example, iron ore was being mined and processed in Pennsylvania. Then again, technological improvements in the iron and steel industry, notably the Gilchrist Thomas process and the Siemens-Marten open-hearth furnace, allowed the use of 'inferior' ores, and so the rich phosphorus-free haematite ore of Furness lost its advantage. And, towards the end of the nineteenth century, some of the richest seams in the district were becoming exhausted. In 1914, the local industry received a warning shot: despite installing electric pumping *on the most up-to-date lines*, the firm of Harrison, Ainslie & Co. went into liquidation in 1914.

The Balmforth 'Coffeepot' on the loading bank at Crooklands. The main line is in the cutting behind the locomotive.
(L&GRP collection courtesy of National Railway Museum, supplied by Peter Holmes)

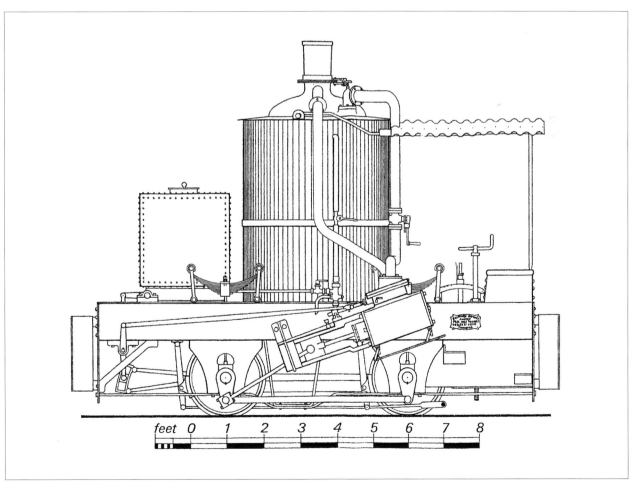

feet 0 1 2 3 4 5 6 7 8

The Balmforth 'Coffeepot', drawn to a scale of 10mm = 1 Foot. *(Drawing by Peter Holmes)*

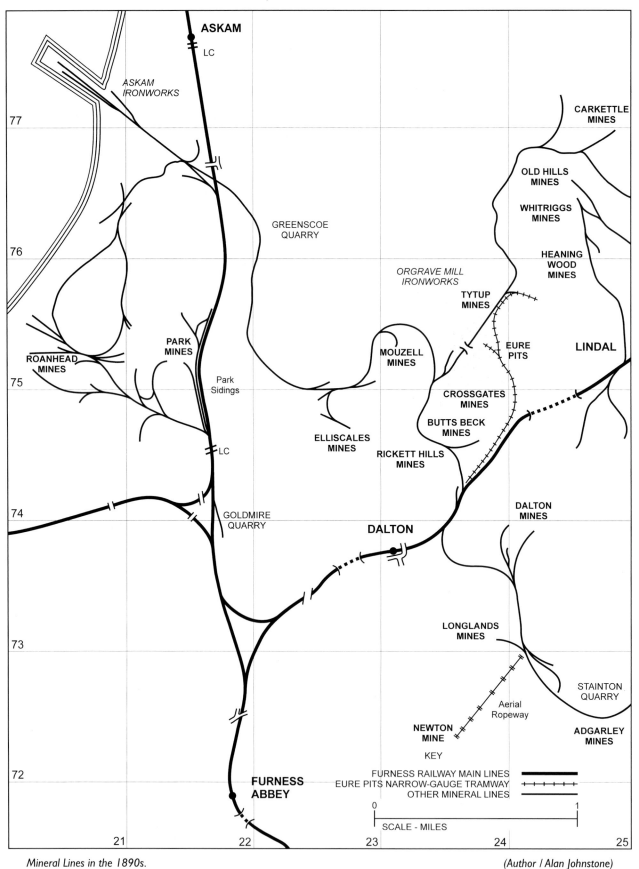

ASKAM
LC

ASKAM
IRONWORKS

77

CARKETTLE
MINES

OLD HILLS
MINES

WHITRIGGS
MINES

GREENSCOE
QUARRY

76

HEANING
WOOD
MINES

ORGRAVE MILL
IRONWORKS

TYTUP
MINES

PARK
MINES

ROANHEAD
MINES

Park
Sidings

MOUZELL
MINES

EURE
PITS

LINDAL

75

CROSSGATES
MINES

ELLISCALES
MINES

BUTTS BECK
MINES

LC

RICKETT HILLS
MINES

GOLDMIRE
QUARRY

74

DALTON
MINES

DALTON

LONGLANDS
MINES

73

STAINTON
QUARRY

Aerial
Ropeway

NEWTON
MINE

ADGARLEY
MINES

KEY

72

FURNESS
ABBEY

FURNESS RAILWAY MAIN LINES
EURE PITS NARROW-GAUGE TRAMWAY
OTHER MINERAL LINES

0   1

SCALE - MILES

21   22   23   24   25

Mineral Lines in the 1890s.   *(Author / Alan Johnstone)*

*Decline in the ore mines; competition for the railway; initiatives during the years of depression;
the Second World War*

*At Nigel Pit, Roanhead, a miner pushes a loaded trolley of ore along a raise to tip it into the loading level below. A miner calls to those below
to warn them, while another miner checks the timbers.* *(Dalton Castle Museum)*

The years of the Great War may have stimulated the demand for iron and steel, but in Furness the heyday of the mining industry was coming to an end. Initiatives there were in plenty, and some of these achieved quite considerable success. While the Park mine closed in 1921, the mine at nearby Roanhead remained in production. The large ore body known as the Rita sop, started around 1875, was not worked out until 1930, while the Nigel sop, discovered by Kennedy Bros in 1902, lasted until July 1942, by which time it had yielded some eleven million tons of ore. At Anty Cross, a new site for mining exploration, BHSC struck ore after sinking a trial shaft in June 1917. The ore was taken by cart to the railway station nearby for transhipment to the ironworks at Barrow. Interestingly, copper was also discovered during the mining operations there. Its importance was not realised at first, the copper being regarded as something of a nuisance. Problems with flooding of the workings caused the mine to be closed in 1928.

Newton Mine & Quarry Co. was formed to explore an area already worked by Schneider and Hannay back in the previous century. These workings were not very deep, and had been abandoned in 1889. The new company, beginning operations in 1904, sank a shaft over 60 fathoms deep, well below the depth of the old workings. This was Woodbine Pit, often called 'Dickie Pink's Pit', Furness ore having a much richer red hue than ore from elsewhere. In 1916, an aerial ropeway was erected, connecting the mine with the Furness Railway's Stainton branch near Longlands. Flooding was always a problem in the mine, particularly over the winter of 1918-19. The lease was reassigned to Newton Mines Ltd, in which the firm of William Beardsmore & Co, Iron & Steel Merchants of Glasgow was the major shareholder, but that did not prevent a succession of misfortunes in 1926. In January the chimney was blown down and had to be replaced, in May there was a delay to production while new electric pumps were installed, and in August the timber lining of the shaft collapsed, fortunately without causing fatalities. With the closure of the Anty Cross mine there was even more water to contend with, and this exacerbated the difficulties. But notwithstanding all this, the mine continued in operation.

The mine workings at Whitriggs had enjoyed a long period of operation, being worked by various companies at different times. BHSC had closed it down in 1914, but three years later it was taken over by North Lonsdale Iron & Steel Co. of Ulverston. They were so inspired by their tonnage returns that in 1922 they decided to take the unprecedented step of relaying the old mineral line from the railway sidings at Lindal station. The level crossing on the main Ulverston road was installed in early September, and from 10 October trains of ore began running down the valley. Sadly, the bad times returned, and, though the company worked it somewhat sporadically, it was eventually abandoned in 1924.

After the Great War, an Act was passed to enable the railways to be re-organised, and so, on 1 January, 1923, the Furness Railway became a constituent of a new company, the London, Midland & Scottish Railway. Inevitably, the war years had taken their toll on the railway, and much work was needed to bring the standard of track and maintenance back up to the level of the pre-war years. In addition, the motor bus was beginning to take to the roads. With newly demobilised servicemen looking for an outlet for their entrepreneurial skills, and with cheap war-surplus vehicles available, it is not surprising that they soon established a network of local routes in many areas, causing the railway companies to view this new competition with some alarm.

In Furness, a group of sixteen owner-drivers set up a co-operative business. Registered on 9 January 1926 and working out of a garage erected in Dalton at the corner of Station Road and Beckside Road, the Furness Omnibus Co. Ltd quickly established itself in the area. One imaginative venture was the introduction of a thrice-weekly service between Barrow and Manchester. The vehicle used for this service was a Leyland Lioness PLC1 (registration number TE1140), which had been fitted with a special body by Hall Lewis, the London firm which was the predecessor of Park Royal. Able to carry twenty-four passengers, it had tables fitted between the seats. The service started on 19 July 1927, but was sadly not a success, and it was discontinued during the winter. Attempts were made to resume the service the following year, operating on Tuesday and Thursday only, but it had finally to be abandoned.

In all its other ventures, the company was a significant success. It acquired the Lonsdale Pullman Bus Co. Ltd in 1928, and the Barrow Bus Co. Ltd (named for its founder, F Barrow) and J Creighton & Sons the following year. By the time it sold out in its turn to Ribble Motor Services in

1930, it was operating on two routes between Barrow and Ulverston, three between Ulverston and Ambleside, a route between Ulverston and Millom, and five local services based on Dalton. The £45,000 purchase price reflected, not only the large number of routes involved, but also the prudent policy the company had of investing in new standard Leyland buses, similar to those which the Ribble company was using. When a new depot was opened in Ulverston in 1933, the Dalton garage remained.

It was as well that Dalton possessed such entrepreneurial spirits, for the depression of the inter-war years was felt as keenly here as anywhere. For the out-of-work, the best chance was to uproot to another part of the country, or, more favourably, abroad, and try to find fame and fortune there. For those who remained, life could be extremely hard. Those in work could expect to toil for long hours in arduous conditions, while for those without, the help available would barely provide for the necessities of life.

Significantly at this time the County Council set up a new school in the town. George Ashburner, who owned the Elliscales estate and carried out mining there, had had a private residence built for himself on land then known as 'Peter Dowdales Field'. In 1880, before he could come to live in Dowdales Mansion, an unexpected failure in the family business investments led him to take his own life. Inhabited by the Kellett family for a short time, and then by Commander Craven, head of Vickers-Armstrongs Ltd of Barrow in Furness, the house was subsequently purchased by the Lancashire County Council which converted it into an educational establishment, opening Dowdales Central School in 1928. This provided specialist teaching for some 40% of the children then attending all-age schools, and the pupils were strongly encouraged to stay on beyond the age of 14, at that time the statutory leaving age.

Tudor Square from Market Street, with a number of the early motor buses in evidence.   *(Sankey 6945)*

Dowdales Mansion, built in the 1890s as a private residence. It was opened as a school in 1928 under its first headmaster, Mr A E Bancroft.
(courtesy James Walton)

With less and less work available in the mines, jobs had to be found further afield. Vickers-Armstrongs owned the shipyard in Barrow, and work here was much sought after, giving better security than the 'temporary employment scheme' offered to the out-of-work. Ore traffic at Crooklands had ceased, and in 1935 the railway company simplified the track layout and closed the signal box.

The Co-operative Society, hopeful for the end of the depression, erected a new building in Market Street. In 'Art Deco' style, it must have struck an odd chord, placed as it was amidst a row of terraced housing. It had departments for furnishing, hardware and ironmongery. It must have appeared very forward looking when it opened in 1935. Window displays showed room settings, with a single suite

Looking up Market Street from its junction with Station Road, before the erection of the new Co-op buildings.
(Sankey 4738)

and set of furniture, instead of the 'pile it high' displays which were then the norm. For many years, Mr Walker was in charge of the Ironmongery Department. His key-cutting skills were legendary, and a 'blank' was never wasted. Customers would come in with a single nail or screw, and ask for 'a dozen like that'. Mr Walker would, after a cursory glance, disappear into the back of the shop, reappearing seconds later with exactly the wanted items. For anyone 'helping out' behind the counter on a Saturday morning, his was a hard act to emulate.

With the outbreak of the Second World War, there was anxiety that Barrow, with its shipyards so important to the war effort, would be a target for bombing raids. As the sirens sounded, Daltonians took refuge 'under the stairs', wondering how accurate the German bombers would be. Barrow suffered one of its major raids on the night of 4-5 May 1941, when German raiders dropped high explosive bombs on the town. Barrow Central station was wrecked, but 'Coppernob', the old 'Bury' locomotive of 1846 which stood in a glass case on the station approach, miraculously survived almost unscathed, with just a shrapnel mark or two as battle scars to show for her ordeal. Rail traffic was considerably disrupted, and it was nearly two weeks before some semblance of normality was restored to the services.

Later in the war, 'daylight nuisance raids' were introduced by the Germans, using a single aircraft and aiming at specific targets. At Roanhead mines, it had been decided that, when an air-raid warning sounded, all movement of men and machinery must immediately cease. This was as a precaution in case the attacking plane, driven away from the very heavily

fortified shipyards at Barrow, might perhaps seek an alternative, easier target. At Nigel Pit one day, Mr Longmire was the 'bogier' for his company of men, and had collected the explosives, detonators, fuses and other items needed. He placed them in the wooden box supplied for the purpose, put the box on the floor of the pit cage and sat on it, ready to enjoy a comfortable ride to the foot of the shaft. About a hundred feet down, the cage came to a stop. An air-raid warning had been received and confirmed. There was a plane buzzing about, and the tophand in charge on the surface was off to find a safe place to shelter. Mr Longmire's thoughts can well be imagined, as he sat on his box containing half a hundredweight of gelignite and a thousand detonators, while up above a German plane was circling, looking for a suitable place to drop its bombs. After what must have seemed an eternity, the voice of the tophand provided a welcome relief when he called down that all was now clear and the cage could be lowered.

As the war progressed, shortages began to be felt. Coal came into the town by rail, and its arrival was eagerly awaited when winter drew in and household stocks were low. Mothers would send their children up to the station to 'see if the coal had come'. If we were in luck, a surreptitious look over the wall in Hollygate Road might show us the coalman filling and weighing his sacks in the yard. He would never have sufficient for all his customers, but he could expect an 'earful' from those he was obliged to miss out!

As the Second World War was being played out on the battlefields of Europe and beyond, little mining activity was going on in Furness. At Roanhead, the Nigel deposit was worked out, and the mine ceased working in July

A general view of Dalton station from near the mouth of Dalton tunnel. Goods yards can be seen on both sides of the line, and in the foreground is a weighbridge for carts to the ore-loading bank. The photograph is from a postcard dated 1904. The large goods shed or warehouse is prominent, and on the island platform are the original canopies with end screens. (courtesy James Walton)

Dalton station in the mid-1930s. The somewhat ramshackle wooden goods shed would survive the Second World War. The tall signals were well-sited for right-hand drive locomotives, but were replaced by conventionally-placed semaphores, the up home signal being positioned on a short post just the other side of the road bridge. (CRA Pattinson collection PA 0082)

Dalton station in the 1960s. The canopy columns are rather thicker than the architect intended (see page 68), probably due to clumsy tracing by an apprentice in the drawing office. (Michael Andrews MAO 2701)

1942. The following month the equipment was auctioned off, nearly eight hundred lots being disposed of in two days. By December, the pits were being dismantled and the shafts capped. At the Woodbine mine, work continued until 1944. When Newton Mines went into liquidation in 1945, surrendering the lease on 31 December, this brought to an end deep shaft mining in Furness. At Whitriggs, a further and final attempt was made to find ore with the opening of a drift mine. J G Wilkinson of Whitehaven started Margaret Mine (named after his wife), and with his foreman, Fred Nott of Swarthmoor, succeeded in gaining a quantity of ore. This rich red ore was deemed unsuitable by the local blastfurnaces, which by now were able to use the harder ores of West Cumberland and elsewhere. With markets difficult to find, this venture came to an end in 1960, the 'Peru of Furness' finally exhausted.

One commodity which was mined successfully for many years was sand. This had been discovered at Yarlside, where iron ore was being obtained by BHSC. The sand found here was particularly suited to foundry work, and a pit, appropriately if unoriginally named Sand Pit, was sunk especially to mine it. Passing to the Abbey Sand Company, production continued right up until 1956.

With the end of the Second World War, it might have been expected that things would rapidly improve. Conditions remained difficult for some years, however, with food rationing in force until the early 1950s. Eventually, things started to pick up, and Daltonians began to hope for a return to more prosperous times.

Limestone quarries around Dalton, looking south-east, as seen from the air. In the foreground is Goldmire Quarry, while beyond the town can be seen the workings of Stainton Quarries. Greenscoe Quarry is out of shot on the left-hand side of the photograph.
(Cumbria & Lancashire Archaeological Unit, courtesy National Monument Record)

The Railway after the Second World War; Building the Bypass; New Facilities for the Town;
Railway Developments

After the war, the brick lining of Dalton Tunnel was found to be showing signs of wear, and of the side walls, erected by James Garden all those years ago, parts were deteriorating. Preliminary investigations had been completed by the middle of 1949, and work on relining the tunnel then began in earnest. It was a long-term project; on 28 November 1951, the North-Western Evening Mail reported:

> *Out of Dalton tunnel has to come a total of about 5,500 cubic yards of masonry, brickwork and 'muck', and into it has to go thousands of bricks .*
> *. .A good deal of effort, imagination, and indeed invention will have gone into the work before relining is complete - perhaps in early 1960!*

The reporter was unduly pessimistic, for, by the summer of 1956, the limestone arches had been enlarged and replaced by brick, the track-gauntletting restored to normal double-line working, the 'restriction' boards removed and the piles of wood baulks and other clutter taken away. Nearly eleven million bricks had been used in the reconstruction. Work then moved to Furness Abbey, where similar relining work continued until 1959.

With iron ore mining having ceased, the sidings at Crooklands saw little activity. The sidings on the up side served the old coal-drops, while on the other side of the line the Stainton branch continued to operate. At one time, sidings had been laid to serve the Dalton Mine, operated by the Dalton Mining Company on the Duke of Buccleuch's land, and also Longlands Mine, again on the Duke's land but operated as part of his Furness Estate. There was also the aerial ropeway which brought ore from the Woodbine Pit, and this ore had also been loaded at these sidings. Now, however, the branch only carried limestone traffic from the Devonshire Quarry at Stainton.

The three photographs on this page show some of the trains that could set spotters' hearts racing. The camera cost ten shillings; the memories are priceless ... On 19 July 1956, just after the completion of work on Dalton tunnel, 'Royal Scot' class 4-6-0 No. 46159 The Royal Air Force eases the evening Manchester-Barrow service out of the station.   (Author)

'Patriot' class 4-6-0 No. 45541 Duke of Sutherland brings the afternoon London-Barrow service under the Ruskinville Bridge on 4 May 1956. Note the immaculate permanent way, the work of the Dalton permanent way gang.   (Author)

Ex-works after overhaul at Crewe Works, 'Royal Scot' class 4-6-0 No. 46124 London Scottish leaves Dalton on 10 August 1956 at the head of the summer 1.30 p.m. Barrow-Crewe.
(Author)

Two private owner wagons, operated by the Dalton-in-Furness Co-operative Society for the carriage of coal, standing at the coal staithes at Crooklands in the mid-1930s. (CRA Pattinson collection PA 1128)

Stainton quarry on 27 August 1961, with passengers on the SLS/MLS railtour inspecting equipment and operations. (CRA HER 030)

Opposite: Class 2F 0-60 No.58116 trundles quietly through Dalton with a train of empties. (Author)

The down goods loop at Dalton was used to gain access to the branch. The locomotive pushed its load of empties up the hill, a short but steep climb. A maximum of twenty wagons had been permitted in Furness Railway days. At the top, the regulator could be eased for the remainder of the run to the quarries. Locomotives observed on the branch during the war years included 22901, 22912 and 3412. A number of ex-Midland Railway Johnson 0-6-0s, classified 2F, mostly with Deeley cabs, were kept at Barrow for this duty. Chimney first, so that the water would run back and ensure the firebox crown remained covered, gravity sanders in use, the noise was fearsome in the close confines of the cutting. The locomotive being at the rear of the train prevented wagons running away down the bank. The favoured locomotive after nationalisation to work the 'Stainton Bobby' turn was 58116.

When Crown Quarry was being worked, the steep descent of 1 in 14 meant that only two wagons could be handled at a time. Devonshire Quarry was an easier proposition, and the loaded wagons, maximum of twenty-four, would be picked up and trundled along the level to the top of the incline. During the Second World War, a short-lived rail system existed in Devonshire Quarry. Operated by BHSC, it connected the quarry face to the primary crushing plant. Two locomotives are known to have worked there, one an 0-4-0 saddle tank manufactured by W G Bagnall Ltd of Stafford in 1896, the other an 0-6-0 saddle tank which Andrew Barclay, Kilmarnock, had produced in 1911. After the war, however, the work was done using Foden dumper trucks. Once the wagons had been picked up, the wagon brakes would be pinned down, and a cautious descent made down the bank to Crooklands. After running round the train, the wagon brakes would be released, and the

locomotive would bring the wagons along the goods loop to Dalton Station signal box, its 'Stainton Bobby' duty done, to await the road to Barrow.

Conditions continued to be difficult in the years following the Second World War. Petrol was still scarce and new motor cars expensive. With so few cars about, children could play in the streets, and no-one's windows were safe. The 1950s were the heyday of the bus. Local services from Dalton served the surrounding villages of Askam, Marton, Newton and Stainton. A frequent service between Barrow and Ulverston passed through the town, and there was a service to Grizebeck. These all saw much use by workers, shoppers, schoolchildren, and by supporters of the rugby and football teams playing at Craven Park and Holker Street. Day trips could be made to Coniston with a change at Ulverston, or to Ambleside, Grange or Kendal, perhaps with a change at Newby Bridge. In the summer, the X99 twice-daily express service from Barrow to Lancaster connected with a network of express services covering the country, and these were well patronised particularly by holidaymakers. With no motorway network, the times were much less favourable than by train, although the fares were considerably cheaper. While the through trains to London needed less than six and a half hours, the daytime coach journey took 13 hours and 52 minutes, with changes at Lancaster and Preston, before arriving at London's Victoria Coach Station. So compared to rail, the coach journey took about twice as long for roughly half the fare.

The railway service was regaining some semblance of normality. The 1 p.m. from Barrow was still the prestige train, offering a through service between Workington and London. In winter, this was 'double-headed', the pilot engine needing to work back to Crewe, its home depot, but in

Fowler Class 4 2-6-4 tank No. 42376 at Crooklands with an evening stopping train for Carnforth. (CRA WOR 085)

summer the engine returned south on another working at 1.30 p.m. from Barrow. This locomotive had arrived in the area the previous evening on a train from Manchester, always a draw for the local 'spotters'. On Thursdays this could be a running-in turn, bringing in 'foreign' engines ex-works after overhaul at Crewe. 'Royal Scots' from Leeds (Holbeck), 'Britannias' from Holyhead, all grist to the mill for the local enthusiasts. The newspaper train still demanded the attendance of paper boys at the station at some unearthly hour of the morning, sorting the newspapers and making the rounds ready for delivery.

And at around a quarter to nine in the evening came the up 'Mail'. This gave the opportunity to post a late written letter, an extra halfpenny stamp ensuring it would arrive with a 'Whitehaven-Preston TPO' postmark. Beginning an overnight journey to London by this service could be an exciting, if not particularly restful, experience, with sleeping car passengers allowed to remain in their berths at Euston until around 7 o'clock the next morning.

Special excursion trains could be seen, some chartered to take local Sunday School children on their annual outing. Haverigg and Lakeside were favourite venues. A strike by

A view from the road bridge, with an up train approaching Crooklands. The signal box is shown to advantage, and the track layout in the vicinity of the station can be clearly seen. (Michael Andrews MAA 68)

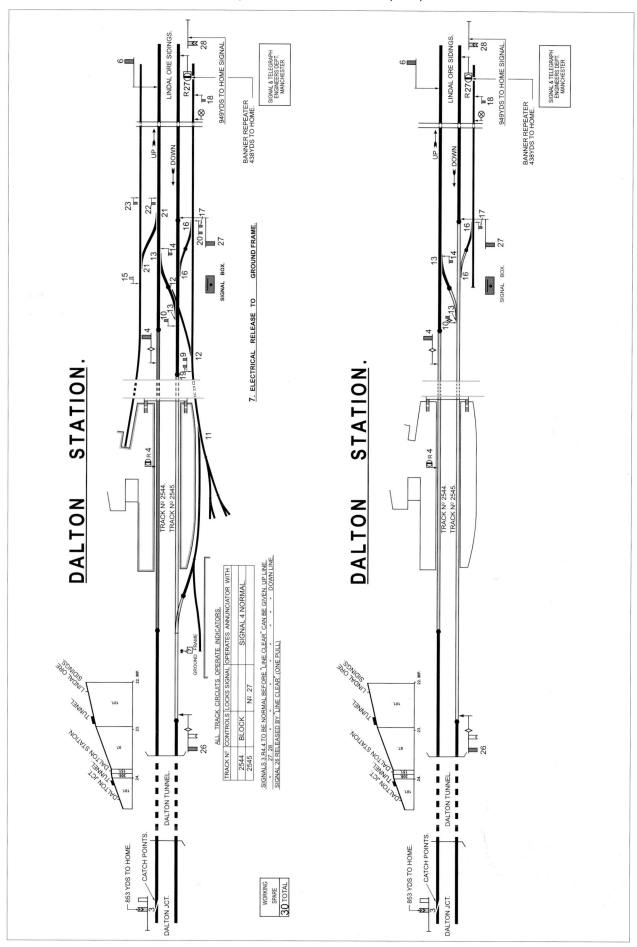

Dalton Station signal box diagrams after the 1940s/50s, and after the closure of the goods yard in 1964. (John Sewell / Alan Johnstone)

Tudor Square today, with the customers of the Black Bull enjoying an afternoon drink. Compare this with the view on page 46. (Author)

Market Place on a peaceful autumn morning. (Author)

bus workers in the summer of 1957 saw Ulverston Grammar School pupils unaccustomedly travelling to Ulverston by train. On one occasion, two Class 5 locomotives at the head of a mere three coaches saw Lindal bank attacked with vigour on the journey home.

As the 1950s gave way to the 1960s, conditions eased. The arrival of the 'Mini' brought motoring within the reach of a much larger section of the population. Construction of Britain's first motorway in 1958, the stretch of the M6 forming the 'Preston Bypass', helped to reduce car journey times, and this was to continue as more and more motorways were built. Bus services suffered as private car traffic increased. Eventually the streets of the town became clogged with parked cars, and a steady hum of vehicles using the main road between Barrow and Ulverston made crossing Market Street extremely hazardous. A bypass had been under consideration before the war. Now the idea surfaced once again. Young mums staged protest marches along Market Street; school pupils carried out traffic surveys. Eventually the government of the day was persuaded to see sense. The new road was cut to the north of the town, leaving the main road on Melton Hill and passing the sites of many of the old iron workings. The Evening Mail carried an article relating how the excavations for the new road had unearthed the old Furness Railway locomotive swallowed up by subsidence in 1892. A photograph of the 'locomotive', an interview with 'Keith Hoakes' and a dateline of 1 April should have been sufficient to reveal that the article was a 'spoof'. The bypass was opened on 17 December 1993 by Dalton's Mayor, Brenda O'Connor, Barrow Council leader, Ted Smith, and Cumbria County Council Chairman Bob Strike. Since then, opportunity has been taken to improve the shopping facilities in the town and to make more attractive the areas around the Castle and Tudor Square.

The Dalton Co-operative Society celebrated its centenary in 1961. An insert in the Dalton News gave a brief illustrated history of the society, from its beginnings in Wellington Street. Sadly, but inevitably, on 2 October 1969, the Committee voted to merge with the Barrow society. Dalton was slowly losing its independence. When local government reorganisation arrived in 1974, Dalton was obliged to bow to the inevitable, and become part of the borough of Barrow-in-Furness, while the whole of the Furness district found itself no longer part of Lancashire but part of Cumbria instead.

Dowdales School, a secondary modern school since 1948, was famously described as 'a unique pocket in English education' when Her Majesty's Inspector visited in 1959. It became a comprehensive school in 1967, and continued the excellent work begun nearly forty years earlier. When in 1984, BBC TV's 'Songs of Praise' team hit town, one cameo showed presenter Geoffrey Wheeler standing in a large hole in the ground. This, he told us, was to be the site of a new swimming pool and leisure centre. It had been the then headmaster of Dowdales, Mr M A Turner, who, recognising a need, had spearheaded a campaign to provide such a facility for the town. The success of the fund-raising appeal was a tribute to the generosity of the people of Dalton and the surrounding district. Their reward was to see the new Swimming Pool and Leisure Centre opened by Princess Margaret on 18 September 1987.

By the time that Dalton folk gathered in St Mary's to sing their 'Songs of Praise', a new church centre had been

Dalton Parish Church, showing the Church Centre, with the restored grave of George Romney in the foreground.   (Author)

Class 47 No. 47 533 leaves Dalton with the 1100 Barrow-Preston on a snowy 26 February 1981. (Author)

A 'Pacer' unit stops at Dalton to allow a solitary passenger to alight. Morecambe hardly seems a tempting destination on such a wintry day as this. These diesel units have recently made a less-than-welcome reappearance on Furness Line trains operated by Northern Rail. (Alan Johnstone)

built, reached through the church's south doorway. Designed by K C White of London, it blends well with its Austin & Paley neighbour, resembling, appropriately enough, a chapter house. While the work disturbed the remains of many former parishioners, necessitating their re-interment, the opportunity was taken to restore completely the grave of George Romney, the portrait painter. Built at a cost of some £120,000, the centre was started in February, 1979, and completed in October, 1980, the dedication being performed by the then Bishop of Carlisle, the Rt Revd David Halsey.

There was anxiety about the future of the railways in the area. The new station at Barrow had opened in 1959, but the iron and steel industry was going through a very difficult period. Through coke trains between Durham and Barrow ceased on 4 July 1960. Becoming part of the Cranleigh Group, the Barrow Ironworks was closed not long afterwards. This deprived the railway of a substantial amount of freight traffic, and led to the closure of the Stainton branch on 12 October 1966. Dalton Station signal

box was also closed on the same day. Closure of the Millom Ironworks was not long in following, the announcement being made in August 1968.

With the end of steam in sight, the Furness line was in at the kill, with some of the last steam workings in the country. It was sad to see large express locomotives little more than a decade old in such a dirty and run-down condition. But this was progress, and by the time Carnforth shed had sent No. 70013 *Oliver Cromwell* on its way with the '15 Guinea Special' on 11 August, 1968, diesel multiple units (DMUs) were operating the local services and main line diesel locomotives were beginning to appear. Among these last were the infamous 'Co-Bos', all of which gravitated to Barrow shed, one of them managing to set the shed on fire.

With more and more freight taking to the roads, the goods facilities were done away with, and the old goods shed in the bay road demolished. The closure was effective from 6 April 1964. The track layout was reduced to merely the up and down lines through the station. The canopies had been leaking rainwater for some years. By now largely

'Jubilee' class 4-6-0 No. 5690 Leander leaves Lindal tunnel with a 'Steam Special' on 31 May 1979. (Author)

Class 47 No. 47 550 stands at the platform with the evening postal and sleeper service on 2 June 1982. The sleeping cars were at the rear. The sorting vans can be seen at the front.   *(Author)*

a decorative feature, they were becoming unsafe, and were removed in 1976. The station had become unmanned on 3 May 1971, along with all other intermediate stations between Barrow and Carnforth with the exception of Grange and Ulverston. The toilets were closed, and desperate passengers made use of the old waiting room on the down platform before that, too, was replaced by an open-fronted shelter. The magazine Lancashire Life featured an article on the town in 1972. Describing Dalton as a 'feisty' town, it was generally very favourable, but bemoaned the lack of a café. It also had some hard things to say about the railway station:

> *Something will need to be done, too, about Dalton's railway station. A few months ago its status was reduced to that of an unmanned halt. Between trains it is an empty, desolate place, its neglected flower beds vividly indicating its demotion, and because there is no supervision the sleepers which formerly made a path across the lines at the end of the platform have been removed. The only way to the opposite platform now is by way of a bridge with steep steps, unusable by the aged and infirm. One lady who has to attend hospital at Barrow once a week is forced to take a train in the opposite direction first to Ulverston station just to cross the line.*

The gloom was lifted a little when British Rail relaxed the 'steam ban' previously imposed on the system. In 1978, regular special excursion trains began running on Furness metals, with Sellafield as the destination, and using large 'Pacific' locomotives from the former 'Big Four' companies

never before seen on the line. That first season saw ex-LNER locomotives No. 4472 *Flying Scotsman* and No. 4498 *Sir Nigel Gresley*. Since then many other preserved locomotives have had the opportunity to tackle Lindal bank and have been seen passing through the town.

'Leaves on the line' is a familiar phrase to today's travellers. On the evening of 17 October 1990, wet leaves conspired with the steep gradients to bring a nuclear flask train to a halt at Dalton tunnel. The train was straddling the catch points, making reversal difficult. The two class 31 locomotives needed assistance before they could restart the train, and services were badly affected.

The scheduled passenger services showed little signs of improvement. The last newspaper train arrived in Barrow on 10 July 1988, ending a 131-year old tradition. The through service to London was axed in 1981, though it was brought back for a short period in the summer of 1985. The last overnight Barrow to London sleeper service ran on 12 May 1990, while the last up mail left Barrow behind 31 425 on the evening of 28 September 1991. Could things get worse under privatisation?

In March of 1997, as part of the privatisation of the rail network, Great Western Holdings Ltd won a seven-year franchise to operate passenger services in the north-west, previously North West Regional Railways. At about the same time, the American-owned English, Welsh and Scottish Railway, which took over most of the freight operations nationally, set about winning back some of the traffic from road. Direct Rail Services, set up as a subsidiary of BNFL at Sellafield to operate nuclear flask trains in the region, also sought to establish their operations.

The franchise for the passenger services was taken over by FirstGroup, successors to Great Western Holdings, in March of 1998. There were initial problems as the new operators made organisational changes and embarked on a damage limitation exercise, facing a financial crisis as the effects of the cuts in subsidy were felt. Reduced services and increased fares became the lot of the passenger, but eventually the new management began to find its feet and started to tackle the problems.

From 12 February, 2001, the train operators, now known as First North Western, began using the new Class 175 'Coradia' units on their Barrow-Manchester Airport services. In preparation for this, it was necessary to 'shave' the platforms to accommodate the extra overhang of these long units. At Dalton station, further refurbishment was undertaken, including a new fence the length of the down platform, resurfacing work and some external footpath reconstruction. A lick of paint contributed to the much-welcomed overall improvement to the station environment. The cost, according to press reports, was £107,000. Alighting from trains at the down platform still required a parachute, for no attempt had been made to raise the platform to a more sensible height. However, disabled passengers were able to reach both platforms without using the overbridge; while it involved a hike into Holygate Road for such passengers from the town who were going to Barrow, it was no longer necessary for them first to travel to Ulverston.

In the summer months, passengers alighting at the station might find a bus service waiting to take them to Dalton's latest tourist attraction, the South Lakes Wild Animal Park. This was begun in 1993 by David Gill, an animal nutritionist, and opened to the public on 28 May 1994. From the start, the Park's visitors marvelled at the freedom that the animals were given in a natural environment. Since then, the Park has continued to expand, a major highlight occurring in 1996 when a Sumatran Tiger took up residence. The miners of an earlier century could scarcely have imagined it.

The Park has a particular involvement with Sumatran Tigers, having set up a trust to fund Sumatran Tiger conservation. This was marked on 19 June 2002 when one of the new 'Coradia' units was named *South Lakes Wild Animal Park – Sumatran Tiger* at Barrow station, attended by First North Western's Commercial Director, Paul Bunting, and by Trust founder and chairman David Gill.

Civic pride was restored to the town in 1987 with the formation of the Dalton with Newton Town Council. When the council met to consider a 'Twin Town', the imaginative decision was taken to look across the Atlantic to America rather than across the Channel to continental Europe, for reasons of common language, heritage, culture and history. Because of population size and location, Dalton, Pennsylvania was chosen as 'Sister City', the twinning taking effect in October 1995. Dalton, Pa. is located in Lackawanna County, near Scranton in north-east Pennsylvania, taking its name from Dr Edward Dalton, a civil war surgeon and superintendent of the New York City Board of Health. Reciprocal visits have been enjoyed by the Mayors of the two towns, and members of Dowdales School and Dalton Town Band have also made the trip across the Atlantic.

On 12 December 2004, Furness found itself with two train operators when FirstGroup plc lost out to Serco-NedRailways for the new Northern Rail franchise. FirstGroup plc had only recently begun operating the TransPennine Express franchise, which included the Barrow to Manchester Airport services. Initially there were teething troubles: Northern Rail took some time to undertake company reorganisation, while TransPennine Express seemed to have as its main priority the avoidance of fines and improvement of punctuality statistics even when this meant missed connections for passengers. In fairness to TPE, the Strategic Rail Authority's National Passenger Survey, carried out in Spring 2005, showed passengers expressing increased overall satisfaction for this franchise holder. TPE are also promising to introduce the

First North Western Commercial Director, Paul Bunting, and Trust founder chairman, David Gill, celebrate the naming of a 'Coradia' unit South Lakes Wild Animal Park - Sumatran Tiger *at Barrow in June 2002.*
(Barrow News and Mail)

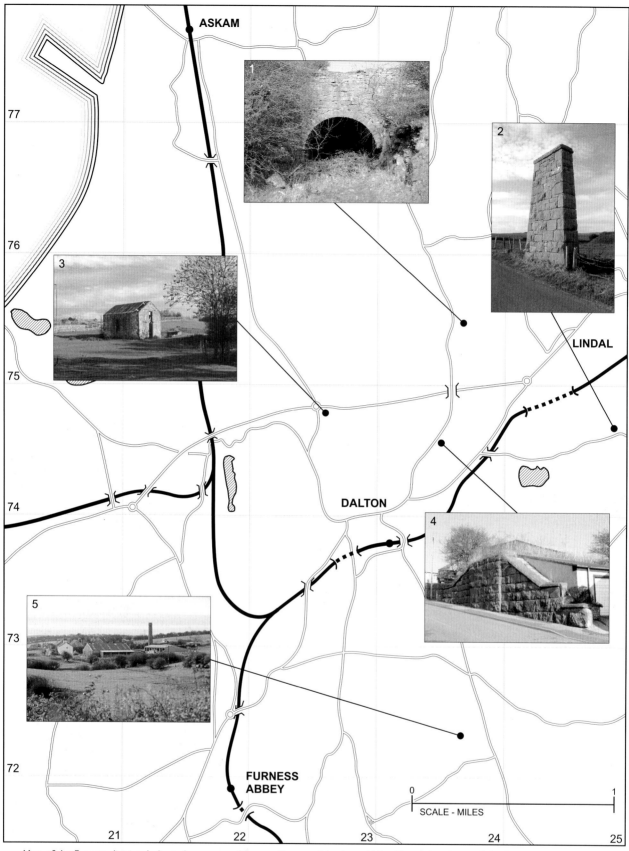

Map of the Furness district. Indicated are some of the readily-accessible sites which still reveal evidence of the district's mining past.
(Author / Peter Holmes / Alan Johnstone)

1   Crossgates tunnel took the Butts tramway on towards High Crossgates. (SD 237 754)
2   Limestone pillar built to carry a tramway over the Urswick road. (SD 249 747)
3   The engine house of Elliscales No. 4 Pit. (SD 226 748)
4   Abutment of the bridge which carried the Butts tramway over the Ireleth road. (SD 234 746)
5   Woodbine Pit chimney, the last remaining iron-ore pit chimney in Cumbria. (SD 236 723)

new fleet of 100 m.p.h. 'Desiro' trains in 2006 (they have already been seen in Furness on driver training runs), and is pressing ahead with a substantial programme of station improvements. It would be good if the two franchise holders quickly learned to work together to their mutual good and to the good of rail users.

Of those mediaeval times, the Abbey of Furness, the ruins carefully looked after and well-maintained by English Heritage, remains for all to see in the Valley of Deadly Nightshade, and looks particularly attractive when the late evening sun glistens on its red sandstone walls. Relics of the mining industry exist, but are less easy to discover. As you climb the hill towards the Wild Animal Park, you will see a bridge abutment on the right-hand side of the road, which once carried the first mineral line from Crooklands to Crossgates. From the crossroads outside Dalton where the Barrow-Stainton road crosses that from Dalton to Newton, the chimney of Woodbine Pit is visible, the last remaining iron ore pit chimney in Cumbria. By the side of the road that leads to Urswick stands a tall limestone pillar built to carry a tramway over the road to the nearby Grievson Pit. Just off the bypass, where it crosses the Askam road near Green Haume Cottages, was a small dilapidated building (reduced to a pile of stones as this book goes to press). You are on the old Elliscales Royalty, and the building was a former engine house from one of the Elliscales mines. It looked over the town of Dalton, enjoying, as the twenty-first century unfolds, as peaceful an existence as at any time in its long and eventful history.

An aerial view of the new bypass, taken on 17 March 1994. The traffic island is at the junction with the Dalton-Askam road, the A595. Beyond, on the far left, is the Wild Animal Park, which opened the following May. On the right of the bypass just beyond the traffic island, is the old Elliscales engine house. The town of Dalton can be seen stretching away on the right-hand side of the picture.
(Cumbria & Lancashire Archaeological Unit, courtesy National Monuments Record)

Acknowledgements

A book is not written without a great deal of help from a good many people, and this over a long period of time. I would like to thank all those who, over the years, wittingly or unwittingly, have contributed anecdote or information, sustained my interest and ultimately helped to see the project through to its conclusion.

In particular:

Dr Peter Holmes (industrial locomotives) and his associate Jonathan Wignall (mineral lines) for much written material in the early days of this project;

Dr Michael Andrews (and his associate Geoff Holme), Les Gilpin, Peter Robinson, John Sewell and my brother John (the professional historian in the family) who read the text when nearly complete and made valuable suggestions;

Alan Johnstone for his computer skills in handling maps, plans and photographs, and turning the author's rough sketches into something more than just acceptable;

Dr Andrews, Geoff Holme, Alan Johnstone, John Sewell, William Wall, Derek Walmsley and James Walton for assistance in the difficult task of selecting photographs;

Dalton with Newton Town Council, and particularly the Town Clerk Mrs H F Thomson and Cllr Ian Singleton for information about the town's heraldic device and other sundry matters;

Jack Gainford for his detailed and careful proof-reading;

Alan Johnstone for typesetting and page layout;

fellow members of the Cumbrian Railways Association Publications Subcommittee, Mike Peascod, Les Gilpin and Alan Johnstone, for their continued encouragement;

my wife Anne for her patience and forbearance.

I am indebted to the Cumbria County Record Offices at Barrow-in-Furness, Kendal and Whitehaven, and to the Local Studies Library, Lancaster. Special thanks are due to the Wolverhampton Archives and Local Studies Library, whose patience and tenacity have allowed me access to a number of rather obscure texts in this and other projects, and who have been a model of what good library practice should be.

I have been able to refer to a number of books, among which I must acknowledge:

Banks, A G: *H W Schneider of Barrow and Bowness* (Kendal, 1984)

Bolton, J: *Geological Fragments of Furness and Cartmel 1869* (Ulverston, 1869)

Dickinson, H W: *John Wilkinson* (Ulverston, 1914)

Fell, A: *The Early Iron Industry of Furness and District* (Ulverston, 1908)

Kelly, D: *The Red Earth* (Barrow, 1998)

McFadzean, A: *The Iron Moor* (Ulverston, 1989)

McGowan Gradon, W: *The Furness Railway* (Altrincham, 1946)

Marshall, J D: *Furness and the Industrial Revolution* (Ilkley, 1958)

Melville, J & Hobbs, J L: *Early Railway History in Furness* (Kendal, 1951)

Richardson, J: *Furness Past and Present* (Barrow-in-Furness, 1880)

Rollinson, W & Harrison, B (ed.): *The Diary of William Fisher 1811 to 1859* (Lancaster, 1986)

Schubert, H R: *History of the British Iron and Steel Industry from c. 450 BC to AD 1775* (London, 1957)

Walton, J: *A History of Dalton-in-Furness* (Chichester, 1984)

West, T: *The Antiquities of Furness 1774* (Reprinted by Michael Moon, Beckermet, 1977)

Cumbrian Railways, the Journal of the **Cumbrian Railways Association**

Transactions of the **Cumberland & Westmorland Antiquarian & Archaeological Society**

- _DALTON STATION_ -

- _UP PLATFORM_ -

RAIL LEVEL

GRADIENT THROUGH STATION 1 in 103.45

ENTRANCE FROM ROAD

ACCESS GATE

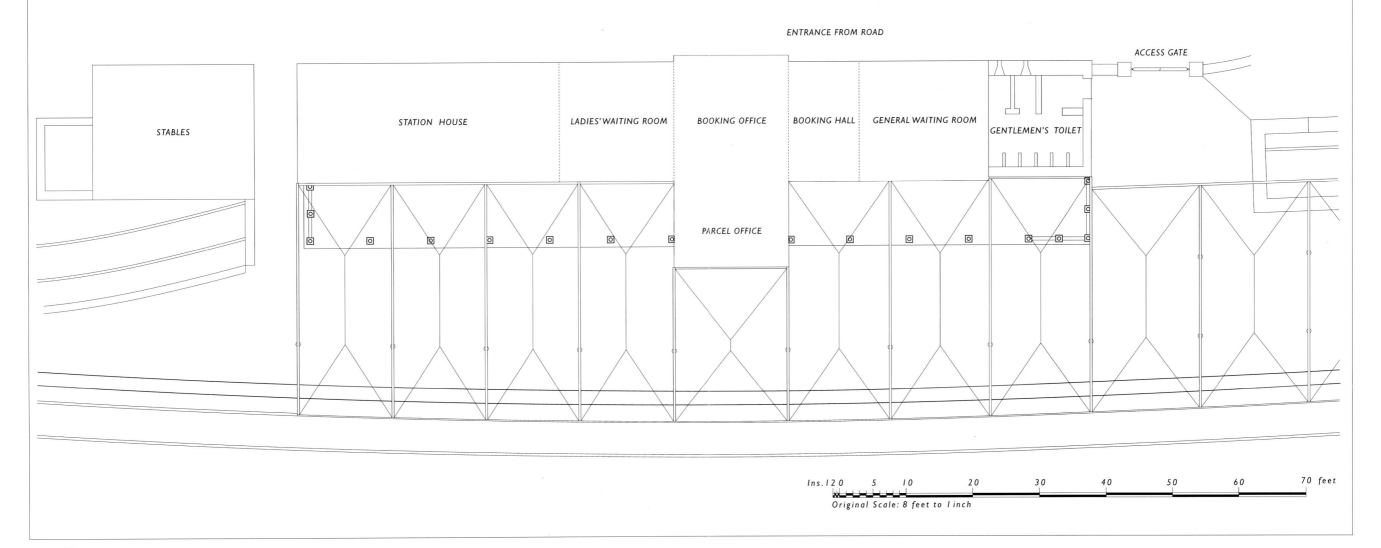

STABLES

STATION HOUSE | LADIES' WAITING ROOM | BOOKING OFFICE | BOOKING HALL | GENERAL WAITING ROOM | GENTLEMEN'S TOILET

PARCEL OFFICE

Ins.120   5   10   20   30   40   50   60   70 feet
Original Scale: 8 feet to 1 inch

On a beautiful spring morning in April 1958, Stanier Class 4 2-6-4T No. 42591 moves the 10.26 a.m. Barrow-Carnforth local service away from Dalton station. (Author)

By 1979 the local services were in the hands of DMUs. On the down platform stands the last remnant of the old Furness Railway buildings which stood on this platform. Used more as a urinal than a waiting room, it had not much longer to go when this photograph was taken. (Author)

The 'Northern Belle' excursion passes through Dalton, hauled by Class 47 No. 47 798 Prince William. (Alan Johnstone AJ-01-0385)

FOLD OUT FOR PLAN AND ELEVATION OF DALTON STATION UP PLATFORM

On a wintry day in 1981, 47 408 leaves Lindal tunnel with the 09.20 Lancaster-Barrow. (Author)

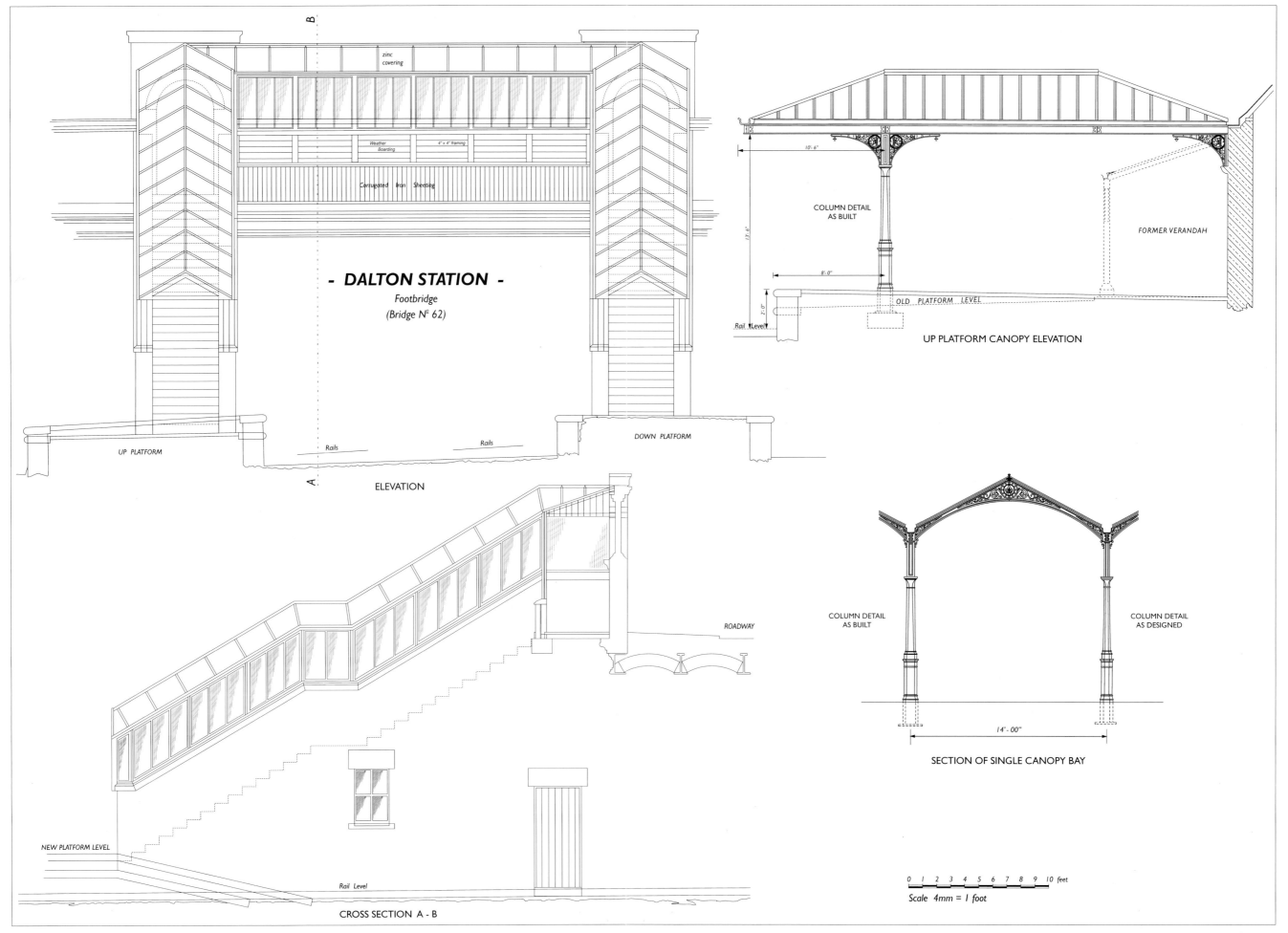

- DALTON STATION -
Footbridge
(Bridge N° 62)

zinc covering

Weather Boarding

4" x 4" framing

Corrugated Iron Sheeting

UP PLATFORM

Rails

Rails

DOWN PLATFORM

B

A

ELEVATION

COLUMN DETAIL AS BUILT

FORMER VERANDAH

10'- 6"

17'- 6"

8'- 0"

3'- 0"

OLD PLATFORM LEVEL

Rail Level

UP PLATFORM CANOPY ELEVATION

ROADWAY

NEW PLATFORM LEVEL

Rail Level

CROSS SECTION A - B

COLUMN DETAIL AS BUILT

COLUMN DETAIL AS DESIGNED

14'- 00"

SECTION OF SINGLE CANOPY BAY

0 1 2 3 4 5 6 7 8 9 10 feet

Scale 4mm = 1 foot

**FOLD OUT FOR PLAN AND ELEVATION OF COVERED FOOTBRIDGE
AND ELEVATIONS OF PLATFORM CANOPY**

On 15 August 2006, 185 108 exits Dalton Tunnel on a special from Grange to Barrow to mark the completion of the Leven viaduct engineering works carried out between 26 March and 16 July 2006. (Dave Garrett)